Learn, Listen & Speak Korean

Master everyday conversations in Korean with 1,000+ essential phrases, pronunciation guide & Hangeul course for fluent communication

Also available:

- Korean Grammar for Beginners (https://geni.us/koreangrammar)
- Korean Short Stories for Beginners (https://geni.us/koreanstories)

Table of Contents

$8 FREE BONUSES

300 USEFUL KOREAN ADJECTIVES and 100 DAYS OF KOREAN WORDS AND EXPRESSIONS E-BOOKS

Inside the 300 Useful Korean Adjectives E-book you will:

- Find a list of 300 commonly used Korean adjectives, each with its English translation.
- Enhance your ability to describe things and express your thoughts and feelings in Korean.
- Improve your vocabulary and understanding of the nuances of the Korean language.

Inside the 100 Days of Korean Words and Expressions E-book you will find:

- A list of useful Korean vocabulary, expressions, and slang terms organized by theme.
- Easy-to-understand English translations for each word and expression.
- A wide range of topics covered, including greetings, travel, food, emotions, and more.

Scan the QR code below to claim your bonuses.

OR

Click the link below:

https://fluentinkorean.com/phrasebook-bonus

Introduction

Welcome to the **"Learn, Listen & Speak Korean"** phrase book!

Whether you are a beginner learner looking to boost your Korean language skills or simply want to review some basic phrases, this book will be a helpful resource.

Inside, you will find a brief introduction to Hangeul, the Korean alphabet, as well as information on syllable blocks, sentence structure, and honorifics. These fundamentals will provide you with the foundation you need to communicate effectively in Korean.

In addition, this book includes over 1,000 essential Korean phrases and vocabulary with English translations, organized into 23 different topics and situations. These phrases are the most up-to-date and relevant for everyday and travel use, and will help you navigate through all the possible scenarios you may encounter as a Korean learner.

To help with your pronunciation, we have included a simple phonetic script for each phrase, as well as high-quality audio recorded by a native Korean speaker. This will help you train your ear to the authentic sound of Korean words and learn to speak naturally. The audio is easy to download, so you can practice anytime, anywhere. The link to download the audio files is available at the end of this book (Page 119).

With its concise and straight-to-the-point topics, this book will be your go-to guide for learning Korean. In addition to being a great tool for those looking to improve their Korean language skills, it can also be a valuable resource for tourists.

Embrace the adventure of learning Korean and immerse yourself in the language and culture—the possibilities are endless!

Sincerely,

The Fluent in Korean Team

PLEASE READ

The link to download the audio files is available at the end of this book. (Page 119)

Korean Alphabet System – Hangeul

Most people say the Korean language is hard, but the Korean alphabet system (**called Hangeul**) is super easy.

Hangeul basics

In Hangeul, there are three basic parts. The first two parts are obligatory; the third part is optional.

Listen to Track 1

A > Obligatory Top Part	Consonant or Consonant Combination (자음) [jaeum]
B > Obligatory Middle Part	Vowel (모음) [mo-eum] or Vowel Composites.
C > Optional Bottom Part	Consonant or Consonant Combination (받침) [bachim] Note: These are the bottom supporting consonant/s.

Example 1: Consonant + Vowel

In this example, the top consonant ㄱ has a "G" sound. The middle vowel, ㅏ has an "ah" sound. So putting it together it sounds like [gah-].

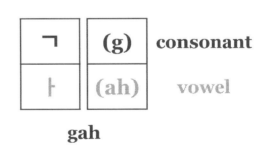

ㄱ	(g)	consonant
ㅏ	(ah)	vowel

gah

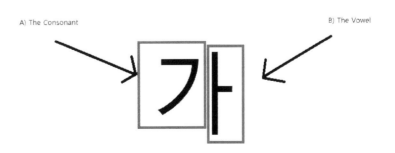

A) The Consonant   B) The Vowel

Example 2: Consonant + Vowel + Consonant

In this example, the top consonant ㄱ has a "G" sound, the vowel ㅏ has an "ah" sound, and the bottom consonant ㄴ has an "N" sound.

Combined together, 간 has the sound of [gahn-]. Why is that? It's because:

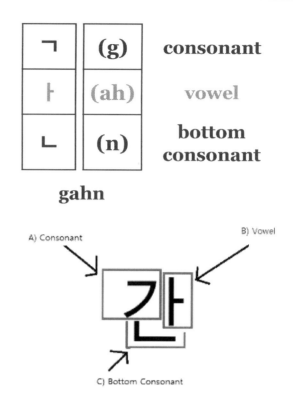

ㄱ	(g)	consonant
ㅏ	(ah)	vowel
ㄴ	(n)	bottom consonant

gahn

A) Consonant   B) Vowel

C) Bottom Consonant

The Basic Consonants

Listen to Track 2

Letter	Korean name	Pronunciation
ㄱ	기역 [giyeok]	G as in "God"
ㄴ	니은 [nieun]	N as in "nose"
ㄷ	디귿 [digeut]	D as in "day"
ㄹ	리을 [rieul]	L as in "shell" or L as in Lala"
ㅁ	미음 [mieum]	M as in "moon"
ㅂ	비읍 [bieup]	B as in "bank" or "bill"
ㅅ	시옷 [siot]	S as in "song" or "say"
ㅇ	이응 [ieung]	O as in "orange" (or no sound – explained later)
ㅈ	지읒 [jieut]	J as in "June"
ㅊ	치읓 [chieut]	Ch as in "cheese"
ㅋ	키읔 [kieuk]	K as in "kick"
ㅌ	티읕 [tieut]	T as in "tiger"
ㅍ	피읖 [pieup]	P as in "pizza"
ㅎ	히읗 [hieut]	H as in "hot"

Hangeul is basically made up of 14 consonants and 10 vowels.

Listen to Track 3

We also have these special ones called **double consonants.** Some consonants can double up to make a more forceful or tensed sound. These kinds of consonants (ㄲ, ㄸ, ㅃ, ㅆ, ㅉ) are called 쌍자음 [ssang-jaeum]. 쌍 [ssang] means "twin." Thus, 쌍자음 (twin-consonants) means that consonants are doubled up to make a more accentuated sound.

Listen to Track 4

Consonant	Korean name	Pronunciation explained
ㄲ	쌍기역 [ssanggiyeok]	가 = gah 까 = ggah
ㄸ	쌍디귿 [ssangdigeut]	다 = dah 따 = ddah
ㅃ	쌍비읍 [ssangbieub]	바 = bah 빠 = bbah
ㅆ	쌍시옷 [ssangsiot]	사 = sah 싸 = ssah
ㅉ	쌍지읒 [ssangjieut]	자 = jah 짜 = jjah

What's the best way to learn these consonants?

Well, have you ever learned the alphabet by singing the alphabet song? The alphabet song is based on "Twinkle Twinkle Little Star."

The Alphabet Song

https://fluentinkorean.com/hangeul-video

Most Korean children learn by singing along to the Korean version of the alphabet song. It's called the **가나다** (gah nah dah) song. The lyrics are as follows:

Lyrics to the Gah-Nah-Dah song:

가 = gah, 나 = nah, 다 = dah, 라 = rah, 마 = mah, 바 = bah, 사 = sah, 아 = aah, 자 = jah, 차 = cha, 카 = ka, 타 = ta, 파 = pa, 하 = ha

Listen to Track 5

ㅏ is a vowel that has an "aah" sound. So, for example:

가나다 (gah nah dah) song

https://fluentinkorean.com/hangeul-video

Once you sing this song multiple times, you'll learn all the basic Korean consonants in no time.

Vowels Explained

There are 21 vowels. We will start with the 10 basic vowels and what they sound like.

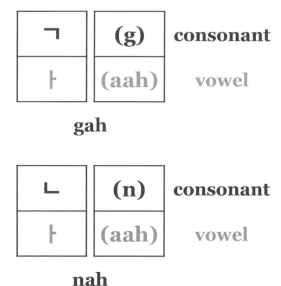

ㄱ	**(g)**	**consonant**
ㅏ	(aah)	vowel

gah

ㄴ	**(n)**	**consonant**
ㅏ	(aah)	vowel

nah

Listen to Track 6

Letter	Korean name	Pronunciation	Example
ㅏ	아	"A" in "Ave Maria"	아침
ㅑ	야	"yah"	야구
ㅓ	어	"ugh" as in someone groaning	어묵
ㅕ	여	"yuh"	여행
ㅗ	오	"oh" as in "orchid"	오빠
ㅛ	요	"yoh"	요리
ㅜ	우	"oo" as in "Uber"	우리
ㅠ	유	"yoo"	유리
ㅡ	으 [eu]	[eu]	음악
ㅣ	이 [i, i-]	"e" as in "eel"	이사

Please note that the consonant "ㅇ" is silent when used as a top consonant. It has an "o" sound when it is used as a bottom consonant.

How to learn the basic vowels

Young Korean children learn the basic Korean vowels by reciting all of the basic vowels at once.

Listen to Track 7

Describing how to pronounce the below set of vowels.

Korean vowels	Pronunciations of these vowels in English	Korean vowels	Pronunciations of these vowels in English
아	aah	요	yo
야	yaah	우	oo
어	uh	유	yoo
여	yuh	으	ui
오	o	이	eeh

The Rest of the Vowels (Compound Vowels):

Compound vowels are composed of two vowels to form a single sound.

Listen to Track 8

Korean Vowel	Combination of	Approximate English pronunciation	Example
ㅐ [ae-]	ㅏ (ah) + ㅣ (eeh)	eh	애인
ㅒ [yae-]	ㅑ (yah) + ㅣ (eeh)	yeh	얘기
ㅔ [e]	ㅓ (ugh) + ㅣ (eeh)	eh	에너지
ㅖ [ye-]	ㅕ (yuh) + ㅣ (eeh)	yeh	예절
ㅘ [wa]	ㅗ (oh) + ㅏ (aah)	wah ("wa" as in Washington)	와인
ㅙ [wae-]	ㅗ (oh) + ㅐ (eh)	weh	왜
ㅚ [oe | we]	ㅗ (oh) + ㅣ (eeh)	weh (there is a slight difference between this and the one above. For the one above you open your mouth slightly wider).	외동

ㅝ [wo ㅣ]	ㅜ(woo) + ㅓ(uh)	wuh (like start pronouncing "woo" then change your mouth to "uh")	워싱턴
ㅞ [we]	ㅜ(woo) + ㅔ(eh)	weh	웨이브
ㅟ [wi]	ㅜ(woo) + ㅣ(eeh)	weeh (like "we" in WeChat)	위하여
ㅢ [ui–]	ㅡ(uuu) + ㅣ(eeh)	uhee (start your mouth with a "uuuuh" then change it to an "eeeh")	의사

It's a bit hard to describe all of these sounds in English, so please be sure to listen to and practice how these consonants and vowels are pronounced from the audio that accompanies this book.

Syllable Blocks

Hangeul is phonetically written, and each syllable gets assigned a block. We call these **syllable blocks**. It is made up of two or more characters (a consonant, a vowel, and an optional final consonant called "**batchim**"). And every word is made up of one or more syllable blocks. We will explain more about "batchim" in the next part of this course.

Note: "C" stands for consonant and "V" for vowel.

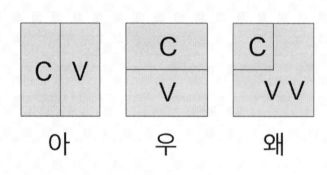

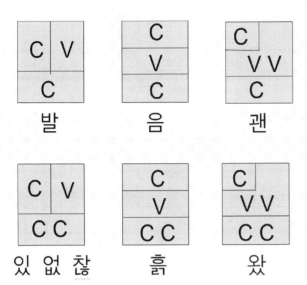

The shape and size of the consonant change depending on what vowel is used. This is to keep the size of each syllable block uniform. The consonant is elongated vertically with the vertical vowel, is elongated horizontally with a horizontal vowel, and becomes smaller when used with a compound vowel.

Now let's take a look at the rest of the syllable blocks.

Final Consonant

Now let's talk about the **final consonant,** the last thing added to the syllable block.

When a Korean syllable ends with a consonant, the consonant is added to that syllable block at the bottom. The final consonant in a syllable is called **받침** [bachim], which literally means "support from underneath."

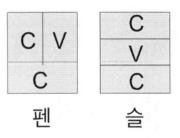

Both of the syllables above end with a consonant. The "n" (ㄴ) is at the bottom of the first syllable, and the "l" (ㄹ) is at the bottom of the second syllable.

The syllable block "원[won]" represents syllables that have consonant + compound vowel + consonant pattern. An example is the word 원 [won], which is the South Korean currency.

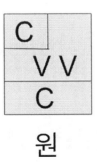

Syllable blocks: Consonant + Vowel + 2 Final Consonants

The last three syllable blocks represent the syllables that end with two consonants, which include the double consonants that we have learned. Some of the words that have syllables ending with two consonants are:

Listen to Track 9

- 밖 [bakk] - *outside*
- 있어요 [issoyo] - *does exist* or *have*
- 없어요 [opssoyo] - *does not exist* or *have not*
- 괜찮아요 [gwaenchanayo] - *It's okay* or *I'm okay*
- 흙 [heuk] - *dirt* or *soil*

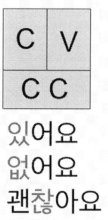

있어요
없어요
괜찮아요

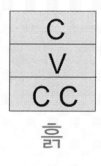

흙

Consonants are tricky because they are pronounced differently depending on whether they are used as the initial or the final consonant (batchim) of a syllable. The general rule of thumb is that the final consonant gets carried over to the vowel sound when followed by a vowel. For example, the original pronunciation of ㄱ is [g]. When ㄱ is followed by a vowel (see "핵이" in the table below), the original sound [g] gets carried over to the vowel that would be pronounced right after the syllable. Also, when followed by the "ㅣ [i]" vowel, some consonants change their pronunciation. For example, the final consonant ㄷ [d] sound changes into a ㅈ [j] sound when followed by the vowel ㅣ [i].

Listen to Track 10

Con-sonant	Consonant name	First consonant pronun-ciation	Final consonant pronun-ciation	Examples			When followed by a vowel		When followed by the vowel [i]
ㄱ	giyeok	g		핵	nuclear	hae**k**	핵이	hae-**gi**	
ㅋ	kieuk	k	k	케이크	cake	kei**k**			
ㄲ	ssanggi-yeok	kk		밖	outside	ba**k**	밖에	ba-**kk**e	
ㄴ	nieun	n	n	안	inside	A**n**	안에	a**n**-ne	
ㄷ	digeut	d		받다	to re-ceive	bat-**d**a	받아	ba-da	bad-**ji**
ㅌ	tieut	t		밭	farm-land, yard	ba**t**	밭에	bba-te	bbat-**chi**
ㅅ	siot	s		맛	flavor	ma**t**	맛이	ma-sh**i**	
ㅆ	ssangsiot	ss	t	탔다	rode (past tense of ride)	tat-**da**	탔어	ta-ss**o**	
ㅈ	jieut	j		잊다	to for-get	it-**da**	잊어	i-juh	
ㅊ	chieut	ch		닻	anchor	da**t**	닻이	da-ch**i**	
ㅎ	hieut	h		좋다	to like	jot-**da**			
ㄹ	ri-ŭl	r	l	길	street	gi**l**	길이	gi-ri	
ㅁ	mieum	m	m	마음	mind	mae-u**m**	마음이	maeu-mi	
ㅂ	bieup	b		밥	rice	ba**p**	밥이	ba-**bi**	
ㅍ	pieup	p	p	앞	front	a**p**	앞에	**a**-peh	
ㅇ	i-ŭng	silent	ng	멍	bruise	me-o**ng**			

Korean Sentence Structure

Let's get started on learning the expressions! To ensure a seamless introduction, let's get acquainted with some of the aspects that will be mentioned constantly.

To begin, Korean sentences are structured in this format: Subject - Object - Verb

Listen to Track 11

Subject		Object		Verb
그	는	사과	를	먹는다
geu	nuˇn	sagwa	ruˇl	meognuˇnda
He		apple		eats

You'll notice that Korean sentences are structured quite differently from English sentences. It will appear odd at first, but you will become accustomed to it as we practice more. One more thing you may have noticed is 는 that follows the subject and 를 that follows the object. You'll also notice that there is no English equivalent for them, which is due to the lack of terms that precisely match them.

This is somewhat comparable to the principle of *a/an/the* in English grammar, which cannot be directly translated into Korean yet we know what they are and what they do.

These are called "topic markers" (은 or 는) and "subject markers" (이 or 가) in Korean. 은 or 이 come after a syllable with a final consonant. 는 or 가 come after a syllable without a final consonant.

Topic Marker

Examples:

Listen to Track 12

밥 [bab], "rice/meal" + 은

그 [geu], "he" + 는

10

The subject marker's primary function is to identify what is being discussed (i.e., the "topic"). Although there is no literal translation, consider it to indicate the phrase "as for [topic]."

For example:

Listen to Track 13

밥은 맛있다 [babeuˇn madittta]: As for the rice/meal, it tastes good.

*밥 - rice or meal / 맛있다 - taste good

그는 선생님입니다 [geunuˇn sonsaengnimimnida]: As for him, he is a teacher.

*그 - he / 선생님 - teacher

Subject Marker

Examples:

Listen to Track 14

강 [gang], "river" + 이

내 [nae], "I" + 가

Similarly, a subject marker appears after a subject to indicate what the topic of the sentence is.

For example:

Listen to Track 15

선생님이 누구예요? [sonsaengnimi nugueyo?]: Who is the teacher?

*선생님 - teacher / 누구 - who

컴퓨터가 고장났다 [kompyutoga gojangnattta]: The computer broke.

*컴퓨터 - computer / 고장났다 - broke (not functioning)

Here are some examples of our expressions that you will be studying later. Determine where they are used and try to become familiar with their usage and nuance.

Listen to Track 16

제 이름은 홍길동입니다.
je ireumeun honggildongimnida.

My name is Hong Gil Dong.

저는 한국인입니다.
joneun hanguginimnida.

I am Korean.

예약이 취소되었어요.
yeyagi chwisodweossoyo.

The reservation was cancelled.

좌석이 몇 번이에요?
jwasogi myot bonieyo?

What number is the seat?

Let's move on to 을 and 를, which follow after the object of a sentence. This element is called the object marker.

Listen to Track 17

Subject		Object		Verb
그	는	사과	를	먹는다
geu	nuˇn	sagwa	ruˇl	meognuˇnda
He		an apple		eat

Object marker

Examples:

Listen to Track 18

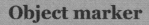
국 [guk], "soup" + 을

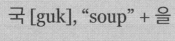
차 [cha], "tea" + 를

Object markers in Korean sentences indicate that a noun is functioning as the sentence's object. Use 을 for syllables that end in a final consonant and 를 for syllables that end in a vowel.

For example:

Listen to Track 19

책을 읽는다 [chaegeuˇl ingnuˇnda]: (I) read a book.

*책 - book / 읽는다 - to read

영화를 본다 [yonghwaruˇl bonda]: I watch a movie.

*영화 - movie / 본다 - to watch

However, in informal speech, they are frequently dropped when the sentence object is evident from the context.

Although this can be a very confusing concept for non-Koreans, you shouldn't be too concerned because Korean people will understand what you're trying to convey even if you mix them up or fail to use them.

Take the time to listen to a variety of Korean expressions and practice by repeating – you'll get the hang of it quickly.

Korean Honorifics

Before you learn to speak Korean, you need to be aware of the varying levels of the spoken language. These different levels are called **honorifics**. Respect is extremely important in Korean culture – respect for age, position, rank, experience, etc. – and hierarchy is interwoven into every aspect of life.

Listen to Track 20

When two Korean people become comfortable with each other, sometimes one person asks the other person for permission to speak to them informally (usually the older person asks the younger person). This is called "letting go of speech" or 말을 놓다. Of course, when you're cursing you should use the informal tone, not the honorific tone. When you're addressing clients, even if they're younger, you should refer to them as 고객님 (esteemed client) or 선생님 (teacher/someone who was born before you/someone you address respectfully).

Example:

"Hello, how are you?"		
Level	Phrase	Romanization
Casual	안녕	annyong
Polite	안녕하세요	annyonghaseyo
Formal	안녕하십니까	annyonghasimnikka

To more about Korean honorifics, please check the article on our website. (https://fluentinkorean.com/korean-honorifics/)

Note:

1. Korean language often omits the subject in a sentence as the verb conjugation and context provide enough information to figure out who or what the subject is. For example, for the English sentence "Is this drama fun?" in Korean you can say "이 드라마 재밌어요?" But if the listener know what are you talking about (this drama), you can say "재밌어요?" without the subject, "이 드라마." This makes communication more concise.

2. Some sentences cannot be translated literally from English to Korean and vice versa. For example, "수고하세요" translated directly to English is "work hard." But it's actually a polite way to express gratitude or appreciation for someone's hard work or effort.

This book contains common, natural expressions and sentences used by Koreans in real-life situations. It will help to improve your fluency and comprehension when communicating with native speakers.

Chapter 1. GREETINGS (인사)

Listen to Track 21 (*Note: The chapter title pronunciation is included in this audio track.*)

안녕하세요. annyeonghaseyo.	**Hello. / Hi.**
저기요! jeogiyo!	**Excuse me! (to catch attention)**
좋은 아침입니다! joeun achimimnida!	**Good morning!**
... 씨 ...ssi	**Mr./Mrs./Ms. ...**
잘 지내요? jal jinaeyo?	**How are you?**
덕분에 잘 지내요. dokppune jal jinaeyo.	**Fine, thanks.**
어떻게 지냈어요? ottoke jinaessoyo?	**How have you been?**
저도 잘 지내요. jodo jal jinaeyo.	**I'm good too.**
이름이 뭐예요? ireumi mwoeyo?	**What's your name?**

제 이름은 (name)입니다.
je ireumeun (name) imnida.

My name is (name).

Listen to Track 22

한국 사람이세요?
hangug saramiseyo?

Are you a Korean?

네.
ne.

Yes.

아니요.
aniyo.

No.

저는 영국 런던 사람이에요.
joneun yongguk rondon saramieyo.

I am English, from London.

한국어 조금 해요. / 한국어 못해요.
hangugeo jogeum haeyo. / hangugeo motaeyo.

I speak a little Korean. / I don't speak Korean.

제 말 이해하세요?
je mal ihaehaseyo?

Do you understand me?

죄송해요. / 미안해요.
jwesonghaeyo. / mianhaeyo.

I'm sorry.

죄송합니다. / 미안합니다.
jwesonghamnida. / mianhamnida.

I apologize.

이해해요.
ihaehaeyo.

I understand.

이해 못해요.
ihae motaeyo.

I do not understand.

조금 더 천천히 이야기해 주세요.
jogeum deo cheoncheonhi iyagihae juseyo.

Please speak more slowly.

다시 말해주실 수 있어요?
dasi malhaejusil ssu issoyo?

Could you repeat that, please?

써주실 수 있어요?
ssojusil ssu issoyo?

Could you write it down, please?

| 영어 하세요?
yeongeo haseyo? | **Do you speak English?** |
| 여기 영어 하시는 분 있으세요?
yeogi yeongeo hasineun bun
isseuseyo? | **Does anyone here speak English?** |

Listen to Track 23

혼자 여행하세요? honja yeohaenghaseyo?	**Are you traveling by yourself?**
저는 혼자 여행 중이에요. joneun honja yohaeng jungieyo.	**I'm traveling alone.**
저는 가족/친구/동료들과 함께 여행 중이에요. joneun gajog/chingu/donglyodeulgwa hamkke yeohaeng jungieyo.	**I'm traveling with my family/ friends/co-workers.**
휴가로/업무로/주말 동안 여기 왔어요. hyugaro/eobmuro/jumal dongan yeogi wassoyo.	**I'm here on holiday / on business / for the weekend.**
만나서 반가워요. / 만나서 기뻐요! mannaseo bangawoyo. / mannaseo gippoyo!	**Nice to meet you. / Pleased to meet you!**
즐거운 여행 되세요! jeulgeoun yeohaengdoeseyo!	**Have a good trip!**
휴가 잘 보내세요! hyuga jal bonaeseyo!	**Enjoy your holiday!**
좋은 하루 보내세요! joeun haru bonaeseyo!	**Have a nice day!**
고맙습니다. / 너무 감사합니다. gomabseubnida. / neomu gamsahabnida.	**Thanks. / Thank you very much.**
별말씀을요. byolmalsseumeulryo.	**You are welcome.**

내일 봐요.
naeil bwayo.

See you tomorrow.

또 봐요.
tto bwayo.

See you again.

잘 지내요!
jal jinaeyo!

Take care!

안녕히 가세요.
annyeonghi gaseyo.

Goodbye. / Bye.

Chapter 2. INTRODUCING YOURSELF (자기소개)

Listen to Track 24 (*Note: The chapter title pronunciation is included in this audio track.*)

이름이 뭐예요? ireumi mwoeyo?	**What's your name?**
제 이름은 피터예요. je ireumeun Petereyo.	**My name is Peter.**
몇 살이에요? myot sarieyo?	**How old are you?**
25살이에요. seumuldasot sarieyo.	**I'm 25 years old.**
어디에서 왔어요? eodieseo wassoyo?	**Where are you from?**
저는 미국/캐나다/영국/ 뉴질랜드에서 왔어요. jeoneun migug/kaenada/yeong-gug/ nyujillaendeueso wassoyo.	**I'm from the USA/Canada/ England/New Zealand.**
저는 영국인/호주인/미국인이에요. jeoneun yonggugin/hojuin/ miguginieyo.	**I'm an English/Australian/ American.**

어디에 살아요?
eodie sarayo?

Where do you live?

저는 런던에 살아요.
jeoneun Londone sarayo.

I live in London.

저희는 뉴욕에 살아요.
jeohuineun nyuyoge sarayo.

We live in New York.

Listen to Track 25

여기 한국 어디에서 머물고 있어요?
yeogi hangug eodieseo meomulgo issoyo?

Where are you staying here in Korea?

저희는 시내 중심에 있는 호텔에 머무르고 있어요.
johineun sinae jungsime inneun hotere momureugo issoyo.

We're staying in a hotel in the city center.

저는 친구와 함께 머물고 있어요.
jeoneun chinguwa hamkke momulgo issoyo.

I'm staying with some friends.

무슨 일 하세요? / 어떤 일 하세요?
museun il haseyo? / otton il haseyo?

What work do you do? / What do you do for a living?

저는 선생님/요리사/회사원이에요.
jeoneun sonsaengnim/yorisa/hwesawonieyo.

I'm a teacher/cook/company employee.

저는 재택근무 해요.
jeoneun jaetaeggeunmu haeyo.

I work from home.

저는 자영업자예요.
jeoneun jayongopjjaeyo.

I'm self-employed.

저는 사업가예요.
jeoneun jayongopjjaeyo.

I'm a businessman/businesswoman.

혹시 결혼하셨어요?
hokssi gyolhonhasyossoyo?

Are you married?

네, 결혼했어요.
ne, gyolhonhaessoyo.

Yes, I'm married.

아니요, 결혼 안 했어요.
aniyo, gyolhon an haessoyo.

No, I'm not married.

이혼했어요.
ihonhaessoyo.

I'm divorced.

Listen to Track 26

저 여자친구 있어요.
jo yeojachingu issoyo.

I have a girlfriend.

저 남자친구 있어요.
jo namjachingu issoyo.

I have a boyfriend.

저는 자녀가 (native Korean number) 명 있어요.
jeoneun janyeoga (number) myong issoyo.

I have (number) children.

저는 자녀가 없어요.
jeoneun janyeoga opssoyo.

I have no children.

여기 얼마나 있을 거예요?
yeogi eolmana isseul kkoeyo?

How long are you going to stay here?

여기 일주일 동안 있을 거예요.
yeogi iljuil dongan isseul kkoeyo.

I'm going to stay here for one week.

핸드폰 번호가 뭐예요?
haendeupon bonhoga mwoeyo?

What is your phone number?

여기 제 전화번호예요.
yogi je jonhwabonhoeyo.

Here's my cell phone number.

연락해요.
yolrakaeyo.

Let's keep in touch.

물론이죠!
mulronijyo!

Sure!

Chapter 3. SCHOOL/EDUCATION (학교/교육)

Listen to Track 27 (*Note: The chapter title pronunciation is included in this audio track.*)

학생이에요? hakssaengieyo?	**Are you a student?**
네. ne.	**Yes, I am.**
어느 학교 다녀요? oneu hakkkyo danyoyo?	**What school do you go to?**
저는 연세대학교 다녀요. joneun yonsedaehakkkyo danyoyo.	**I go to Yonsei University.**
전공이 뭐예요? jongongi mwoeyo?	**What is your major?**
뭐 전공해요? mwo jongonghaeyo?	**What major are you in?**
간호학을 공부하고 있어요. ganhohageul gongbuhago issoyo.	**I'm studying nursing.**
제 전공은 건축학이에요. je jongongeun gonchukagieyo.	**My major is architecture.**

저는 경영학 전공하고 있어요. jeoneun gyeongyeonghag jeongonghago issoyo.	**I'm majoring in business administration.**
몇 학년이에요? myot hangnyonieyo?	**What year are you in?**
저는 2학년이에요. jeoneun i hangnyonieyo.	**I'm in my second year.**
졸업까지 몇 년이나 남았나요? jol-eobkkaji myeoch nyeon-ina nam-assnayo?	**How many more years before you graduate?**
3년 더 남았어요. sam nyon do namassoyo.	**Three more years.**

Listen to Track 28

전공에서 뭐가 제일 좋아요? jongongeso mwoga jeil joayo?	**What do you like the most about your major?**
어떤 과목을 잘해요? otton gwamogeul jalhaeyo?	**What subjects are you good at?**
저는 수학을 잘해요. joneun suhageul jalhaeyo.	**I'm good at math.**
대학교에서 뭐를 제일 좋아해요? daehakkkyoeso mworeul jeil joahaeyo?	**What do you like the most about university?**
대학이 고등학교보다 더 어려워요? daehagi godeunghaggyoboda deo oryowoyo?	**Is college more difficult than high school?**
네, 더 어려워요. ne, do oryowoyo.	**Yes, it is more difficult.**
일주일에 수업 몇 번 가요? iljjuire suop myot bon gayo?	**How many times a week do you have to go to classes?**
저희는 일주일에 다섯 번 가야 돼요. johineun iljjuire dasot bon gaya dwaeyo.	**We need to go five times a week.**
한 학기에 몇 과목 들어요? han hakkkie myot gwamok deuroyo?	**How many subjects do you take in a semester?**

약 6과목이요.
yak yosot gae gwamogiyo.

Around 6 subjects.

대학 졸업하고 계획이 뭐예요?
daehak joropago gyehwegi mwoeyo?

What is your plan after you finish college?

회사에 지원할 거예요.
hwesae jiwonhal kkoeyo.

I will apply for a company.

석사 학위 준비할 거예요.
sokssa hagwi junbihal kkoeyo.

I will prepare for my master's degree.

Chapter 4. SHOPPING (쇼핑)

Listen to Track 29 (*Note: The chapter title pronunciation is included in this audio track.*)

쇼핑 가고 싶어요. syoping gago sipoyo.	**I want to go shopping.**
(object)을/를 어디에서 살 수 있나요? (object) eul/reul eodieseo sal ssu innayo?	**Where can I buy (object)?**
…에서 살 수 있어요 …eso sal ssu issoyo	**You can buy it at …**
백화점 baeghwajeom	**a department store**
옷가게 osgage	**a clothing store**

신발가게 sinbalgage	a shoe store
보석가게 bosokkkage	a jewelry store
무엇을 도와드릴까요? mueoseul dowadeulilkkayo?	May I help you?
무엇을 찾고 계시나요? mueoseul chatkko gyesinayo?	What are you looking for?
(object) 을/를 찾고 있어요. (object) eul/ruel chatkko issoyo.	I'm looking for (object).

Listen to Track 30

티셔츠 tisyocheu	a t-shirt
바지 baji	pants
치마 chima	a skirt
원피스 wonpisseu	a dress
블라우스 beulrausseu	a blouse
양복 yangbok	a suit
스웨터 seuwaeto	a sweater
코트 koteu	a coat
재킷, 잠바 jaekit, jamba	a jacket
잠옷 jamot	pajamas

속옷 sogot	**underwear**
스타킹 seutaking	**stockings**
수영복 suyongbok	**a swimming suit**

Listen to Track 31

양말 한 켤레 yangmal han kyolre	**a pair of socks**
신발 한 켤레 sinbal han kyolre	**a pair of shoes**
운동화 undonghwa	**sneakers**
슬리퍼 seulripo	**slippers**
우산 usan	**an umbrella**
향수 hyangsu	**perfume**
손목시계 sonmokssigye	**a watch**
악세사리 akssesari	**accessories**
선글라스 ssongeulrasseu	**sunglasses**
모자 moja	**a hat, a cap**
손수건 sonssugon	**a handkerchief**
가방 gabang	**a bag**

넥타이 nektai	**a necktie**
장갑 janggap	**gloves**

Listen to Track 32

그거 볼 수 있나요? geugo bol su itnayo?	**Can I look at it?**
그것 좀 보여주세요. geugot jom boyeojusaeyo.	**Please show me that.**
여기 있습니다. yeogi issseubnida.	**Here it is.**
이거 입어봐도 돼요? / 해봐도 돼요? igo ibobwado dwaeyo? / haebwado dwaeyo?	**May I try this on? / Can I try it on?**
사이즈가 어떻게 되세요? ssaijeuga ottoke dweseyo?	**What is your size?**
스몰/미디엄/라지요. seumol/midiom/rajiyo.	**My size is small/medium/large.**
어디에서 입어볼 수 있어요? odieso ibobol ssu issoyo?	**Where can I try it on?**
잘 맞아요. jal majayo.	**It fits me well.**
너무 작아요. / 너무 커요. neomu jagayo. / neomu keoyo.	**It's too small. / It's too big.**
안 맞아요. an majayo.	**It doesn't fit.**
마음에 들지 않아요. maeume deulji anayo.	**I don't like it.**
마음에 들어요. maeume deuroyo.	**I like it.**
이걸로 할게요. igolro halkkeyo.	**I'll take it.**

제가 찾던 거예요.
jega chattton goeyo.

That's what I was looking for.

Listen to Track 33

얼마예요?
olmaeyo?

How much is it?

부가세가 포함되어 있나요?
bugassega pohamdweo innayo?

Is the tax included?

너무 비싸요.
nomu bissayo.

It is very expensive.

좀 깎아주실 수 있어요?
jom kkakkajusil ssu issoyo?

Could you give me a discount?

좀 더 싼 거 있나요?
jom deo ssangeo itnayo?

Do you have something cheaper?

다른 것들도 보여주시겠어요?
daleun geosdeuldo boyojusigessoyo?

Could you show me some others?

어디에서 계산해요?
odieso gyesanhaeyo?

Where do I pay?

어떻게 계산하시겠어요?
eotteohge gyesanhasigesseoyo?

How do you want to pay?

현금으로 할게요.
hyeongeum-eulo halkkeyo.

I'll pay in cash.

신용카드 / 체크카드 돼요?
sinyongkadeu / chekeukadeu dwaeyo?

Do you accept credit cards/debit cards?

여기 10,000원이요.
yogi manwoniyo.

Here is 10,000 won.

쇼핑백 필요하세요?
ssyopingppaek piryohaseyo?

Do you need a shopping bag?

Listen to Track 34

잔돈 드릴게요.
jandon deurilkkeyo.

Here is your change.

영수증 여기 있습니다.
yeongsujeung yeogi issseubnida.

Here is your receipt.

환불하고 싶어요.
hwanbulhago sipoyo.

I'd like a refund.

이거 교환할 수 있어요?
gyohwanhal ssu issoyo?

Can I exchange this?

간식 좀 사고 싶어요.
gansigeul sago sipoyo

I want to buy some snacks.

여기 근처에 편의점 있나요?
yogi geunchoe pyonijom innayo?

Is there a convenience store near here?

식료품이 필요해요.
singnyopumi piryohaeyo.

I need some groceries.

제일 가까운 마트가 어디예요?
jeil gakkaun mateuga odieyo?

Where is the nearest supermarket?

야채 코너가 어디예요?
yachae koneoga odieyo?

Where is the vegetable section?

비닐 어디에 있어요?
binil odie issoyo?

Where is the plastic bag?

삼겹살 100그램에 얼마예요?
samgyopssal baekkkeuraeme olmaeyo

How much is 100 grams of pork belly?

2킬로 주세요.
ikilro juseyo.

2 kilos, please.

계산대가 어디예요?
gyesandaega odieyo?

Where is the checkout?

봉투 필요하세요?
bongtu piryohaseyo?

Do you need a bag?

Chapter 5. AT THE RESTAURANT (식당에서)

Listen to Track 35 (*Note: The chapter title pronunciation is included in this audio track.*)

여기 근처에 괜찮은 식당 있어요? yogi geunchoe gwaenchaneun sikttang issoyo?	**Is there a good restaurant around here?**
채식주의자가 갈만한 식당이 있나요? chaesikjjuijaga galmanhan sikttangi innayo?	**Is there a restaurant that vegetarians can go to?**
오늘 저녁 예약할 수 있나요? oneul bam sigsaga ganeunghalkkayo?	**Can I make a reservation for dinner tonight?**
몇 분이세요? myot buniseyo?	**For how many people?**
네 명이요 ne myongiyo.	**Four, please.**
방 있나요? bang innayo?	**Do you have a private room?**
창가 쪽 테이블로 주세요. changkka jjok teibeulro juseyo.	**I'd like a table by the window.**

여기요. / 저기요. yeogiyo. / jeogiyo.	Here, please. / Excuse me there. (to call a waiter)
메뉴판 좀 주세요. menyupan jom juseyo?	Can you bring the menu, please?
영어 메뉴판 있나요? yongo menyupan innayo?	Do you have a menu in English?

MENU

오늘의 요리 : 부대찌개 – 공깃밥과 다섯 가지 반찬 포함. 12,000원 oneure yori : budaejjigae - gonggitppapkkwa dasot gaji banchan poham. manichonwon	Today's dish: Budaejjigae - with rice and five side dishes. 12,000 won
점심 특선 : 한우 갈비탕 – 소갈비와 무를 넣어 몇 시간 동안 끓인 맑은 탕 jomsim teuksson : hanu galbitang - sogalbiwa mureul noo myot sigan dongan kkeunin malgeun tang	Lunch Special: Korean Beef Rib Soup - Clear soup made of beef ribs simmered for a few hours with radish and garlic

Listen to Track 36

주문하시겠어요? jumunhasigessoyo?	May I take your order?
뭐 드릴까요? mwo deurilkkayo?	What would you like?
추천 좀 해주세요? chuchon jom haejuseyo?	What would you recommend?
뭐가 제일 맛있어요? mwoga jeil madissoyo?	What's the best dish?
오늘의 요리가 뭐예요? oneure yoriga mwoeyo?	What is the dish of the day?
뭐가 같이 나와요? mwoga gachi nawayo?	What does it come with?

이걸로 주세요. igeolo juseyo.	**I'll have this.**
주문할게요. jumunhalgeyo.	**I would like to order.**
전채요리 / 애피타이저 jeonchaeyoli / aepitaijo	**starter/appetizer**
샌드위치 saendeuwichi	**sandwich**
국/탕 gug/tang	**soup**
치킨 chikin	**fried chicken**
소고기 구이 sogogi gui	**roast beef**

Listen to Track 37

스테이크 seuteikeu	**steak**
새우 saeu	**shrimp**
야채 샐러드 / 채소 샐러드 yachae saelleodeu / chaeso saelleodeu	**vegetable salad**
빵 ppang	**bread**
파스타 paseuta	**pasta**
초밥 chobap	**sushi**
김밥 gimppap	**gimbap (dried seaweed rolls)**
김치볶음밥 gimchibokkeumbap	**kimchi-bokkeumbap (kimchi fried rice)**

돌솥비빔밥 dolsotppibimppap	**dolsot-bibimbap (sizzling stone pot bibimbap)**
불고기덮밥 bulgogidopppap	**bulgogi-deopbab (bulgogi with rice)**
산채비빔밥 sanchaebibimppap	**sanchae-bibimbap (mountain vegetable bibimbap)**
쌈밥 ssambap	**ssambap (rice with leaf wraps)**
오징어덮밥 ojingodopppap	**ojingeo-deopbap (spicy sauteed squid with rice)**

Listen to Track 38

콩나물국밥 kongnamulgukppap	**kongnamul-gukbap (bean sprout soup with rice)**
잣죽 jatjjuk	**jat-juk (pine nut porridge)**
전복죽 jonbokjjuk	**jeonbok-juk (rice porridge with abalone)**
호박죽 hobakjjuk	**hobak-juk (pumpkin porridge)**
만두 mandu	**mandu (Korean dumplings)**
물냉면 mulraengmyon	**mul-naengmyeon (cold noodles in chilled broth)**
비빔국수 bibimgukssu	**bibim-guksu (spicy noodles)**
비빔냉면 bibimnaengmyon	**bibim-naengmyeon (spicy cold noodles)**
수제비 sujebi	**sujebi (hand-torn noodle soup)**
잔치국수 janchigukssu	**janchi-guksu (Korean noodle soup, banquet noodles)**

쟁반국수 jaengbangukssu	**jaengban-guksu (cold spicy platter noodles)**
칼국수 kalgukssu	**kalguksu (knife-cut noodle soup)**
갈비탕 galbitang	**galbitang (beef rib soup)**

Listen to Track 39

감자탕 gamjatang	**gamjatang (pork back-bone stew)**
곰탕 gomtang	**gomtang (beef bone soup)**
된장국 dwenjangkkuk	**doenjangguk (soybean paste soup)**
떡국 ttokkkuk	**tteokguk (sliced rice cake soup)**
떡만둣국 ttongmandutkkuk	**tteok-mandutguk (sliced rice cake and mandu soup)**
만둣국 mandutkkuk	**mandutguk (mandu soup)**
매운탕 maeuntang	**maeuntang (spicy fish stew)**
미역국 miyokkkuk	**miyeokguk (seaweed soup)**
북엇국 bugotkkuk	**bugeotguk (dried pollack soup)**
설렁탕 solrongtang	**seolleongtang (ox bone soup)**
육개장 yukkkaejang	**yukgaejang (spicy beef soup)**
해물탕 haemultang	**haemultang (spicy seafood stew)**

Listen to Track 40

김치찌개 gimchijjigae	**kimchi-jjigae (kimchi stew)**
된장찌개 dwenjangjjigae	**doenjang-jjigae (soybean paste stew)**
부대찌개 budaejjigae	**budae-jjigae (spicy sausage stew)**
순두부찌개 sundubujjigae	**sundubu-jjigae (soft tofu stew)**
청국장찌개 chonggukjjangjjigae	**cheonggukjang-jjigae (rich soybean paste stew)**
곱창전골 gopchangjongol	**gopchang-jeongol (beef tripe hot pot)**
신선로 sinnonno	**sinseollo (royal hot pot)**
갈비찜 galbijjim	**galbijjim (braised short ribs)**
삼계탕 samgyetang	**samgyetang (ginseng chicken soup)**
보쌈 bossam	**bossam (napa wraps with pork)**
수육 suyuk	**suyuk (boiled beef or pork slices)**
아귀찜 agwijjim	**agwijjim (braised spicy monkfish)**

Listen to Track 41

족발 jokppal	**jokbal (pigs' feet)**
해물찜 haemuljjim	**haemuljjim (braised spicy seafood)**

도토리묵 dotorimuk	**dotorimuk (acorn jelly salad)**
잡채 japchae	**japchae (sweet potato starch noodles stir fried with vegetables)**
불고기 bulgogi	**bulgogi**
삼겹살 samgyopssal	**samgyeopsal (grilled pork belly)**
닭갈비 dakkkalbi	**dakgalbi (spicy stir-fried chicken)**
한정식 hanjongsik	**hanjeongsik (Korean set menu)**
2인분 주세요. iinbun juseyo.	**Two servings, please.**
이거 하나, 이거 둘 주세요. igo hana, igo dul juseyo.	**One of these and two of these, please.**
너무 맵지 않게 해주세요. nomu maepjji anke haejuseyo.	**Not too spicy, please.**

Listen to Track 42

굽기는 어떻게 해드릴까요? gupkkineun ottoke haedeurilkkayo?	**How would you like it cooked?**
미디엄 레어로 해주세요. midiom reoro haejuseyo.	**Medium rare, please.**
사이드로 구운 야채 주세요. ssaideuro guun yachae juseyo.	**I would like grilled vegetables on the side.**
어린이용 식사 있나요? oriniyong sikssa innayo?	**Do you have children's meals?**
채식주의자 메뉴 있나요? chaesikjjuija menyu innayo?	**Do you have a vegetarian menu?**
고기 없는 메뉴가 뭐예요? gogi omneun menyuga mwoeyo?	**Which menu has no meat?**

생선이 없는 요리가 뭐예요?
saengseon-i eobsneun yoliga mwoeyo?

Which dishes have no fish?

계란 빼주세요.
gyeran ppaejuseyo

Please remove the eggs.

저 유제품 알러지 있어요.
jo yujepum alroji issoyo.

I'm allergic to dairy.

저 해산물 알러지 있어요.
jo haesanmul alroji issoyo.

I'm allergic to seafood.

저 견과류 알러지 있어요.
jo gyongwaryu alroji issoyo.

I'm allergic to nuts.

Listen to Track 43

음료는 안 필요하세요?
eumnyoneun an piryohaseyo?

Would you like anything to drink?

커피 할게요.
kopi halkkeyo.

I'll have coffee.

녹차 주세요.
nogcha juseyo.

Green tea, please.

아니요, 괜찮아요.
aniyo, gwaenchanayo.

No, I am fine.

오렌지 주스 한 잔이요.
olenji juseu han janiyo.

A glass of orange juice, please.

병맥주랑 생맥주 중에 뭐
드릴까요?
byongmaekjjurang saengmaekjju
junge mwo deurilkkayo?

What would you like, bottled beer or draft beer?

생맥주로 주세요.
saengmaekjjuro juseyo.

I'd like a draft beer, please.

소주 한 병 주세요.
soju han byeong juseyo.

I like to have a bottle of soju.

화이트 와인 한 병 주세요.
hwaiteu wain han byeong juseyo.

I would like a bottle of white wine, please.

레드 와인 한 잔 주세요.
redeu wain han jan juseyo.

One glass of red wine, please.

디저트는 뭐로 하시겠어요?
dijoteuneun mworo hasigessoyo?

What would you like for dessert?

Listen to Track 44

치즈 케이크 주세요.
chijeu keikeu juseyo

Cheese cake, please.

초콜릿 아이스크림 할게요.
chokolrit aiseukeurim halkkeyo.

I will have chocolate ice cream.

얼마나 기다려야 돼요?
olmana gidaryoya dwaeyo?

How long do we have to wait?

너무 배고파요.
nomu baegopayo.

I'm very hungry.

빨리 부탁드려요.
ppalri butaktteuryoyo

Please serve us quickly.

목말라요.
mongmalrayo.

I'm thirsty.

주문하신 음식 나왔습니다.
jumunhasin eumsig nawassseubnida.

Here is your order.

식사 맛있게 하세요!
sigsa maditkke haseyo!

Enjoy your meal!

잘 먹겠습니다.
jal mokkketsseumnida.

Thank you for the meal.

저 이거 주문 안 했어요.
jo igo jumun an haessoyo.

I did not order this.

이거 샐러드로 바꿔 주실 수 있어요?
igo ssaelrodeuro bakkwo jusil ssu issoyo?

May I change this for a salad?

맥주가 안 시원해요. 시원한 걸로 주시겠어요?
maekjjuga an siwonhande siwonhan golro jusigessoyo?

This beer isn't cold. Could you give me a cold one?

Listen to Track 45

물 좀 더 주시겠어요? mul jom do jusigessoyo?	Could I have some more water, please?
배불러요. baebulroyo.	I'm full.
잘 먹었습니다. jal mogotsseumnida	I enjoyed the meal.
음식이 맛있어요. eumsigi madissoyo.	The food is delicious.
남은 것 좀 포장해 주세요. nameun got jom pojanghae juseyo.	Please wrap up the leftovers.
계산서 좀 주세요. gyesanso jom juseyo.	The bill, please.
계산은 카운터에서 도와드릴게요. gyesaneun kauntoeso dowadeurilkkeyo.	I'll help you with the payment at the counter.
계산이 잘못된 것 같아요. gyesani jalmotttwen got gatayo.	There is a mistake in the bill.
이 가격은 뭐예요? i gagyogeun mwoeyo?	What are these charges for?
영수증 필요하세요? yongsujeung piryohaseyo?	Do you need a receipt?
잔돈은 괜찮아요. jandoneun gwaenchanayo.	Keep the change.
음식하고 분위기 다 너무 좋았어요. eumsikago bunigi da nomu joassoyo.	The food and atmosphere were all great.

Chapter 6. AT THE AIRPORT (공항에서)

Listen to Track 46 (*Note: The chapter title pronunciation is included in this audio track.*)

공항에 어떻게 가요? gonghange ottoke gayo?	**How do I get to the airport?**
공항 가는데 얼마나 걸려요? gonghang ganeunde olmana golryoyo?	**How long does it take to get to the airport?**
1터미널로 가야 돼요. iltominolro gaya dwaeyo.	**We have to go to Terminal 1.**
이 터미널은 국제선이에요. i tominoreun gukjjesonieyo.	**This terminal is for international flights.**
여기는 국내선 터미널이에요. yogineun gungnaeson tominorieyo.	**This is the domestic terminal.**
표 어디에서 사요? pyo odieso sayo?	**Where can I buy tickets?**
인천행 두 장 주세요. inchonhaeng du jang juseyo.	**Two tickets to Incheon please.**
어느 항공사예요? oneu hanggongsaeyo?	**Which airline is this?**

직항이에요?
jikangieyo?

Is this a direct flight?

체크인 카운터는 어디에 있어요?
chekeuin kauntoneun odie issoyo?

Where are the check-in counters?

인천행 체크인은 어디에서 해요?
inchonhaeng chekeuineun odieso haeyo?

Where do I check-in for Incheon?

Listen to Track 47

항공권과 여권 보여주세요.
hanggongkkwongwa yokkwon boyojuseyo.

Please show me your airline ticket and passport.

부치실 짐 있으세요?
buchisil jim isseuseyo?

Do you have any baggage to check?

네, 캐리어 두 개 있어요.
ne, kaerio du gae issoyo.

Yes, I have two suitcases.

휴대용 가방 몇 개 있으세요?
hyudaeyong gabang myot gae isseuseyo?

How many carry-on bags do you have?

이거 하나요.
igo hanayo.

This one.

기내에 들고 타도 돼요?
ginaee deulgo tado dwaeyo?

Can I carry it on board?

몇 킬로까지 괜찮아요?
myot kilrokkaji gwaenchanayo?

How many kilograms is okay?

무게 제한을 넘었어요.
muge jehaneul nomossoyo.

Your luggage exceeds the weight limit.

초과 비용을 지불하시거나 짐을 줄여주세요.
chogwa biyongeul jibulhasigona jimeul juryojuseyo.

Please pay for the excess cost or reduce your luggage.

초과 비용이 얼마예요?
chogwa biyongi olmaeyo?

How much is the fee for excess baggage?

Listen to Track 48

자리를 변경/선택할 수 있나요? jarireul byongyongsontaekal ssu innayo?	Can I change/choose my seat?
창가 좌석과 복도 좌석 중 어디를 원하십니까? changkka jwasokkkwa boktto jwasok jung odireul wonhasimnikka?	Would you like a window or an aisle seat?
통로 자리가 좋아요. tongno jariga joayo	I prefer an aisle seat.
창가 자리요. changkka jariyo.	A window seat please.
탑승권 여기 있습니다. 좋은 비행 되세요. tapsseungkkwon yogi itsseumnida joeun bihaeng dweseyo.	Here's your boarding pass. Have a nice flight.
인천행 출발 게이트가 어디예요? inchonhaeng chulbal geiteuga odieyo?	Where is the departure gate for Incheon?
2번 게이트에서 탑승해 주세요. ibon geiteueso tapsseunghae juseyo.	Please board at gate 2.
탑승 몇 시에 시작해요? tapsseung myot sie sijakaeyo?	What time will the boarding start?
탑승은 약 10분 후에 시작됩니다. tapsseungeun yak sipppun hue sijakttwemnida.	Boarding will begin in approximately ten minutes.
탑승권 보여주세요. tapsseungkkwon boyojuseyo.	Show me your boarding pass, please.
탑승권을 잃어버렸어요. tapsseungkkwoneul iroboryossoyo.	I lost my boarding pass.

Listen to Track 49

탑승이 약 10분 뒤에 종료됩니다. tapsseungi yak sipppun dwie jongnyodwemnida.	Boarding will close in approximately ten minutes.

비행기가 지연되었습니다.
bihaenggiga jiyondweotsseumnida.

Your flight is delayed.

얼마나 지연되나요?
olmana jiyondwenayo?

How long will it be delayed?

항공편이 취소되었습니다.
hanggongpyoni
chwisodweotsseumnidaa.

Your flight is canceled.

짐 찾으려면 어디로 가야 돼요?
jim chajeuryomyon odiro gaya
dwaeyo?

Where can I claim my luggage?

인천에서 출발한 비행기 수하물은
어디 있어요?
inchoneso chulbalhan bihaenggi
suhamureun odi issoyo?

**Where is the luggage for the
flight from Incheon?**

인천에서 온 비행기 짐은 어디로
나와요?
inchoneso on bihaenggi jimeun odiro
nawayo?

**Where does the luggage from
Incheon come out?**

제 짐이 아직 안 나왔어요.
je jimi ajik an nawassoyo.

My luggage hasn't come out yet.

제 짐이 분실 됐어요.
je jimi bunsil dwaessoyo.

My luggage has been lost.

이 호텔로 가는 공항버스가
있나요?
i hotelro ganeun gonghangpposseuga
innayo?

**Is there an airport bus to this
hotel?**

Chapter 7. On the Plane (비행기에서)

Listen to Track 50 (*Note: The chapter title pronunciation is included in this audio track.*)

제 자리 찾는 것 좀 도와주시겠어요? je jari channeun got jom dowajusigessoyo?	**Would you please help me find my seat?**
좌석 번호가 어떻게 되십니까? jwasok bonhoga ottoke dwesimnikka?	**What is your seat number?**
이쪽으로 앉으세요. ijjogeuro anjeuseyo.	**This way, please.**
자리를 바꿀 수 있을까요? jarireul bakkul ssu isseulkkayo?	**Would it be possible to change seats?**
저... 일행과 함께 앉고 싶은데요. jo ilhaenggwa hamkke ankko sipeundeyo.	**Well... My partner and I would like to sit together.**
일행과 바꿔드릴게요. ilhaenggwa bakkwodeurilkkeyo.	**I can switch places with your partner.**
정말 감사해요. jeongmal gamsahaeyo.	**Thanks a lot.**

죄송합니다만, 제 자리에 계신 것 같은데요.
jwesonghamnidaman je jarie gyesin got gateundeyo.

I'm sorry, I think you're in my seat.

제 좌석이에요.
je jwasogieyo.

That's my seat.

제 탑승권을 확인해 볼게요.
je tapsseungkkwoneul hwaginhae bolkkeyo.

Let me check my boarding pass.

죄송해요, 제 실수예요.
jwesonghaeyo, je silssueyo.

I'm sorry, my mistake.

괜찮습니다.
gwaenchansseumnida.

It's alright.

괜찮아요.
gwaenchanayo.

No problem.

Listen to Track 51

이 가방, 선반에 넣는 것 좀 도와주시겠어요?
i gabang, sonbane nonneun got jom dowajusigessoyo?

Could you help me put this bag in the overhead compartment?

물론이죠.
mulronijyo.

Sure.

가장 가까운 비상구는 어디예요?
gajang gakkaun bisangguneun odieyo?

Where is the nearest emergency exit?

가장 가까운 출구는 바로 여기입니다.
gajang gakkaun chulguneun baro yogiimnida.

Your nearest exit is right here.

가장 가까운 화장실은 어디예요?
gajang gakkaun hwajangsireun odieyo?

Where is the nearest lavatory?

가장 가까운 화장실은 바로 저기에 있습니다. gajang gakkaun hwajangsireun baro jogie itsseumnida.	**The nearest lavatory is right there.**
만약 산소마스크가 필요하면요? manyak sansomaseukeuga piryohamyonnyo?	**What if I need an oxygen mask?**
산소 마스크는 머리 위에 있고 필요하다면 아래로 떨어질 것입니다. sanso maseukeuneun mori wie itkko piryohadamyon araero ttorojil kkosimnida.	**The oxygen mask is above your head and will drop down if you need it.**
구명조끼는 어디에 있나요? gumyongjokkineun odie innayo?	**Where are the life jackets?**
구명조끼가 필요하면 좌석 밑에서 찾을 수 있습니다. gumyongjokkiga piryohamyon jwasok miteso chajeul ssu itsseumnida.	**You will find your life jacket under your seat if you need it.**
손님 여러분, 출발 준비가 되었습니다. sonnim yorobun chulbal junbiga dweotsseumnida.	**Ladies and gentlemen, we are ready for departure.**
자리에 앉아주세요 jarie anjajuseyo.	**Please take your seat.**
좌석 벨트를 매주세요. jwasok belteureul maejuseyo.	**Please fasten your seatbelt.**
이륙을 앞두고 있으니 휴대전화 전원을 꺼주세요. iryugeul apttugo isseuni hyudaejonhwa jonwoneul kkojuseyo.	**Please switch off your mobile phone as we are about to take off.**

Listen to Track 52

안녕하세요. 닭고기, 소고기, 생선 중 어느 것을 드시겠습니까?
annyonghaseyo dakkkogi sogogi saengson jung oneu goseul deusigetsseumnikka?

Hello sir. Would you like chicken, beef, or fish?

치킨으로 할게요.
chikineuro halkkeyo.

I will have the chicken.

메뉴 좀 봐도 될까요?
menyu jom bwado dwelkkayo?

May I see the menu?

음료 마실 수 있을까요?
eumnyo masil ssu isseulkkayo?

Can I have a drink?

물, 커피, 탄산음료, 와인 중 어느 것을 원하십니까?
mul kopi tansaneumnyo wain jung oneu goseul wonhasimnikka?

Do you want water, coffee, soda, or wine?

더 필요한 건 없으세요?
do piryohan gon opsseuseyo?

Would you like to have anything else?

담요 좀 주시겠어요?
damnyo jom jusigessoyo?

Can I have a blanket, please?

여기 있습니다.
yogi itsseumnida.

Here you go.

더 필요한 건 없으신가요?
do piryohan gon opsseusingayo?

Is there anything else that I can get you?

아니요, 괜찮습니다.
aniyo, gwaenchansseumnida.

No, thanks.

좋은 비행 되세요.
joeun bihaeng dweseyo.

Have a nice flight.

Chapter 8. VISA AND IMMIGRATION (비자 및 입국)

Listen to Track 53 (*Note: The chapter title pronunciation is included in this audio track.*)

세관/여권 검사는 어디에 있습니까? segwanyokkwon gomsaneun odie itsseumnikka?	**Where is customs / passport control?**
여권과 비자를 보여주세요. yokkwongwa bijareul boyojuseyo.	**Please show me your passport and visa.**
여권 좀 볼 수 있을까요? yeogwon jom bol su isseulkkayo?	**Can I see your passport?**
여기 제 여권입니다. yogi je yokkwonimnida.	**Here is my passport.**
어떤 비자를 가지고 있나요? otton bijareul gajigo innayo?	**What kind of visa do you have?**
여행 오셨나요 아니면 사업차 오셨나요? yohaeng osyonnayo animyon saopcha osyonnayo?	**Are you a tourist or here on business?**
저는 관광 비자/학생 비자/사업 비자를 가지고 있습니다. joneun gwangwang bija/hakssaeng bija/saop bijareul gajigo itsseumnida.	**I have a tourist/student/business visa.**

한국에 오신 목적이 무엇입니까? hanguge osin mokjjogi muosimnikka?	**What is the purpose of your visit here in Korea?**
저는 여기에 휴가/공부/업무를 위해 왔습니다. joneun yogie hyugagongbuommureul wihae watsseumnida.	**I'm here on holiday / to study / for business purposes.**
저는 혼자 여행 중입니다. joneun honja yohaeng jungimnida.	**I'm traveling on my own.**
저는 남편과 여행 중입니다. joneun nampyongwa yohaeng jungimnida.	**I'm traveling with my wife/ husband.**
저는 아들/딸과 함께 여행 중입니다. joneun adeul/ttalgwa hamkke yohaeng jungimnida.	**I'm traveling with my son/ daughter.**

Listen to Track 54

여행 일정을 보여주세요. yohaeng iljjongeul boyojuseyo.	**Please show me your itinerary.**
증명 서류를 보여주세요. jeungmyong soryureul boyojuseyo.	**Please show me your supporting documents.**
여기 한국에 얼마나 머무르실 건가요? yogi hanguge olmana momureusil kkongayo?	**How long will you stay here in Korea?**
3일 동안 있을 겁니다. samil dongan isseul gomnida.	**I'm here for three days.**
2주 동안있을 겁니다. iju dongan isseul gomnida.	**I'm here for two weeks.**
어디에서 머무르십니까? odieso momureusimnikka?	**Where are you going to stay?**
저는/우리는 통통 쁘띠 호텔에 머물 거예요. joneunurineun tongtong ppeutti hotere momul kkoeyo.	**I/We will stay in Tong Tong Petit Hotel.**

신고하실 물건이 있나요?
singohasil mulgoni innayo?

Do you have anything to declare?

신고할 것 없습니다.
singohal kkot opsseumnida.

I have nothing to declare.

음식물을 가져왔나요?
eumsingmureul gajowannayo?

Have you brought any food into the country?

아뇨, 없습니다.
anyo, opsseumnida.

No, nothing.

입국이 승인/거부 되었습니다.
ipkkugi seungin/gobu
dweotsseumnida.

Your entry is approved/denied.

한국에 오신 것을 환영합니다.
hanguge osin goseul
hwanyonghamnida.

Welcome to Korea.

Chapter 9. TAKING THE TAXI (택시 타기)

Listen to Track 55 (*Note: The chapter title pronunciation is included in this audio track.*)

택시를 타고 싶은데요. taekssireul tago sipeundeyo.	**I would like to take a taxi.**
어디서 택시를 탈 수 있나요? odiso taekssireul tal ssu innayo?	**Where can I get a taxi?**
택시를 불러 주시겠어요? taekssireul bulro jusigessoyo?	**Could you order me a taxi?**
가능한 빨리 택시를 타고 싶어요. ganeunghan ppalri taekssireul tago sipoyo.	**I would like a taxi as soon as possible.**
오후 8시에 택시를 타고 싶어요. ohu yodolssie taekssireul tago sipoyo.	**I would like a taxi at 8 p.m.**
여기서 기다려 주세요. yogiso gidaryo juseyo.	**Wait here, please.**
타세요. taseyo.	**Get in.**
몇 분이세요? myot buniseyo?	**How many are you?**

승객 4명만 탈 수 있어요. seunggaek nemyongman tal ssu issoyo.	**I can only take 4 passengers.**
가방을 트렁크에 넣어드릴까요? gabangeul teurongkeue noodeurilkkayo?	**Shall I put your bag in the trunk?**

Listen to Track 56

어디 가세요? eodigaseyo?	**Where are you going?**
시내로 가주세요. sinaero gajuseyo.	**Please take me to the city center.**
이 주소로 가주세요. i jusolo ga juseyo.	**Please take me to this address.**
거기는 몰라요. 지도 있어요? gogineun molrayo. jido issoyo?	**I don't know that place. Do you have a map?**
이 지도로 보여 주시겠어요? i jidoro boyo jusigessoyo?	**Can you show me on this map?**
멀어요? moroyo?	**Is it far?**
아주 가까워요. aju gakkawoyo.	**It is very close.**
꽤 멀어요. kkwae moroyo.	**It is pretty far away.**
20분 정도 걸릴 거예요. isipppun jongdo golril kkoeyo.	**It will take about 20 minutes.**
더 빠른 길/지름길을 이용해 주세요. do ppareun gil/jireumkkireul iyonghae juseyo.	**Please take the faster route/ shortcut.**
급하세요? geupaseyo?	**Are you in a hurry?**
급해요. geupaeyo.	**I'm in a hurry.**

Listen to Track 57

조심히/천천히 운전해주세요. josimhi/chonchonhi unjonhaejuseyo.	**Please drive carefully/slowly.**
안전벨트 매세요. anjonbelteu maeseyo.	**Put on your seat belt, please.**
미터기 사용하나요? mitogi sayonghanayo?	**Do you use your meter?**
시내까지 가는데 얼마 나와요? sinaekkaji ganeunde olma nawayo?	**How much is it going to cost to go to the city center?**
10,000원 정도 나올 거예요. manwon jongdo naol kkoeyo.	**It would cost around 10,000 won.**
혼잡 시간이에요. honjap siganieyo.	**It's rush hour.**
차가 밀려요. chaga milryoyo.	**There's a traffic jam.**
다른 길로 가볼게요. dareun gilro gabolkkeyo.	**I'll try a different way.**
창문 열어도 될까요? changmun yorodo dwelkkayo?	**Is it okay if I open a window?**
에어컨을 켤/끌 수 있나요? eokoneul kyol/kkeul ssu innayo?	**Can you please turn on/off the AC?**
목적지에 도착했나요? mogjeogjie dochaghaessnayo?	**Have we reached our destination?**

Listen to Track 58

다음 신호등에서 세워주세요. daeum sinhodeungeso sewojuseyo.	**Stop at the next traffic light, please.**
여기 세워주세요. yeogi sewojuseyo.	**Stop here, please.**
여기에서 내릴게요. yogieso naerilkkeyo.	**I will get out here.**

얼마예요?
olmaeyo?

How much is it?

12,000원 나왔습니다.
manichonwon nawatsseumnida.

The meter shows ₩12,000.

더 작은 돈 있나요?
do jageun don innayo?

Do you have smaller notes/bills?

죄송한데, 제가 잔돈이 없어요.
jwesonghande, jega jandoni opssoyo.

Sorry, I don't have any change.

거스름돈은 괜찮아요.
goseureumttoneun gwaenchanayo.

Keep the change.

팁 감사합니다.
tip gamsahamnida.

Thank you for the tip.

안전운행 감사합니다.
anjonunhaeng gamsahamnida.

Thanks for the safe ride.

미터기 요금보다 많아요.
mitogi yogeumboda manayo.

It's more than on the meter.

사기꾼!
sagikkun!

Swindler!

Chapter 10. TAKING THE SUBWAY (지하철 타기)

Listen to Track 59 (*Note: The chapter title pronunciation is included in this audio track.*)

가장 가까운 지하철역이 어디예요? gajang gakkaun jihacholryogi odieyo?	**Where's the nearest subway station?**
근처에 지하철역 있나요? geunchoe jihacholryok innayo?	**Is there a subway station nearby?**
지하철역은 저쪽이에요. jihacholryogeun jojjogieyo.	**The subway station is that way.**
역 이름이 뭐예요? yok ireumi mwoeyo?	**What is the name of this station?**
여기는 강남역이에요. yogineun gangnamnyogieyo.	**This is Gangnam station.**
지하철 노선도 있으세요? jihachol nosondo isseuseyo?	**Do you have a map of the subway?**
성수역까지 어떻게 가요? songsuyokkkaji ottoke gayo?	**How do I get to Seongsu station?**
어느 쪽이 강남역방향이에요? oneu jjogi gangnamnyokppanghyangieyo?	**Which way is towards Gangnam Station?**

어느 역에서 내려야 돼요? oneu yogeso naeryoya dwaeyo?	**Which station should I get off at?**
세 번째 역에서 내리세요. se bonjjae yogeso naeriseyo.	**Get off at the third station.**
명동역까지 몇 개 남았어요? myongdongnyokkkaji myot gae namassoyo?	**How many stops are left until Myeongdong Station?**

Listen to Track 60

명동역에 가려면 갈아타야 하나요? myongdongnyoge garyomyon garataya hanayo?	**Do I have to transfer to get to Myeongdong Station?**
몇 호선으로 갈아타야 돼요? myot hosoneuro garataya dwaeyo?	**Which line should I switch to?**
지하철 표 어디에서 사요? jihachol pyo odieso sayo?	**Where can I buy a subway ticket?**
저기, 발매기에서요. jogi balmaegiesoyo.	**Over there, at the ticket vending machine.**
저기, 표 사는 것 좀 도와주세요. jogi, pyo saneun got jom dowajuseyo.	**Excuse me, please help me buy a ticket.**
교통카드 충전 어디에서 해요? gyotongkadeu chungjonhago sipoyo?	**Where can I recharge my transportation card?**
발매기나 편의점에서 할 수 있어요. balmaegina pyonijomeso hal ssu issoyo	**You can do it at the ticket vending machine or at the convenience store.**
만 원 충전해 주세요. man won chungjonhae juseyo.	**Please add 10,000 won.**
역무실이 어디예요? yongmusiri odieyo?	**Where is the station office?**
전철에 가방을 두고 내렸어요. jonchore gabangeul dugo naeryossoyo.	**I left my bag on the train.**

Listen to Track 61

열차가 들어오고 있습니다. yolchaga deuroogo itsseumnida.	**The train is approaching.**
승강장 사이가 넓으니 타실 때 주의하시기 바랍니다. seunggangjang saiga nolbeuni tasil ttae juihasigi baramnida.	**Please watch your step, the gap between train and platform is wide.**
이번역은 홍대입구역입니다. ibonnyogeun hongdaeipkkuyogimnida.	**This stop is Hongik University Station.**
내리실 문은 왼쪽입니다. naerisil muneun waenjjogimnida.	**The doors are on your left.**
다음 역이 어디예요? daeum yogi odieyo?	**What is the next station?**
다음은 신촌역이에요. daeumeun sinchonnyogieyo.	**Next is Sinchon Station.**
시청역에 언제 도착하는지 알려주실 수 있으세요? sichongnyoge onje dochakaneunji alryojusil ssu isseuseyo?	**Could you tell me when I arrive at City Hall Station?**
여기에서 내리세요. yogieso naeriseyo.	**This is your stop.**
감사합니다. 안녕히 가세요. gamsahamnida. annyonghi gaseyo.	**Thank you. Bye.**

Listen to Track 62 (*Note: The chapter title pronunciation is included in this audio track.*)

좋은 호텔을 찾고 있습니다. joeun hotereul chatkko itsseumnida.	**I am looking for a good hotel.**
저렴한 호텔을 찾고 있어요. joryomhan hotereul chatkko issoyo.	**I am looking for an inexpensive hotel.**
이 근처에 좋으면서도 저렴한 호텔을 추천해주실 수 있으세요? i geunchoe joeumyonsodo joryomhan hotereul chuchonhaejusil ssu isseuseyo?	**Can you recommend a good, cheap hotel around here?**
저는 시내 중심 근처에 있고 싶어요 . joneun sinae jungsim geunchoe itkko sipoyo.	**I want to be near the town center.**
예약했어요. yeyakaessoyo.	**I have a reservation.**
방 하나 예약하고 싶어요. bang hana yeyakago sipoyo.	**I'd like to book a room, please.**

제 이름은 (name)이에요.
je ireumeun (name)ieyo.

My name is (name).

빈 방 있나요?
bin bang innayo?

Do you have an available room?

1인실 있어요?
irinsil issoyo?

Do you have a single room?

2인실 있나요?
iinsil innayo?

Do you have a double room?

스위트룸 있어요?
seuwiteurum issoyo?

Do you have a suite?

Listen to Track 63

이틀 밤 묵고 싶은데요.
iteul bam mukkko sipeundeyo.

I'd like to stay for two nights.

7월 2일부터 7월 6일까지요.
chirwol iilbuto chirwol yugilkkajiyo.

From July 2 to July 6.

하루에 요금이 얼마예요?
harue yogeumi olmaeyo?

What is the rate per day?

세금이 포함되어 있나요?
segeumi pohamdweo innayo?

Are taxes included?

현금으로 계산할 수 있나요?
hyongeumeuro gyesanhal ssu innayo?

Can I pay in cash?

신용카드/체크카드 받나요?
sinyongkadeu/chekeukadeu bannayo?

Do you accept credit cards/debit cards?

방을 보고 싶은데요.
bangeul bogo sipeundeyo.

I would like to see the room.

제 방 번호가 뭐예요?
je bang bonhoga mwoeyo?

What is my room number?

43번 방입니다.
sasipssambon bangimnida.

Room number 43.

방 키 주세요.
bang ki juseyo.

My room key, please.

승강기는 어디에 있나요? seunggganggineun odie innayo?	**Where is the elevator?**
엘리베이터가 있나요? elribeitoga innayo?	**Is there an elevator?**

Listen to Track 64

좋아요. 할게요. joayo. halkkeyo.	**It's fine. I'll take it.**
이 방은 마음에 들지 않아요. i bangeun maeume deulji anayo.	**I don't like this one.**
룸서비스 부탁합니다. rumssobisseu butakamnida.	**Room service, please.**
음식을 주문하고 싶은데요. eumsigeul jumunhago sipeundeyo.	**I would like to order food.**
제 방에 수건이 없어요. je bange sugoni opssoyo.	**There are no towels in my room.**
욕실에 뜨거운 물이 안 나와요. yokssire tteugoun muri an nawayo.	**There's no hot water in the bathroom.**
매니저와 이야기하고 싶어요. maenijowa iyagi hago sipoyo.	**I would like to speak to the manager.**
담요 한 장 더 받을 수 있나요? damnyo han jang do badeul ssu innayo?	**Can I get another blanket?**
수영장 사용할 수 있나요? suyongjang sayonghal ssu innayo?	**Can I use the swimming pool?**
(7)시에 깨워주세요. (ilgop)sie kkaewojuseyo.	**Please wake me at (seven).**
제 방에서 아침 식사하고 싶은데요. je bangeso achim sikssahago sipeundeyo.	**I want breakfast in my room.**

Listen to Track 65

방 청소 좀 해주세요. bang chongso jom haejuseyo.	**Please clean up my room.**
체크아웃은 몇 시예요? chekeuauseun myot sieyo?	**What time is checkout?**
내일까지 여기에 짐 보관해도 될까요? naeilkkaji yogie jim bogwanhaedo dwelkkayo?	**May I store baggage here until tomorrow?**
제 돈을/열쇠를 깜빡했어요. je doneul/yolsswereul kkamppakaessoyo.	**I forgot my money/keys.**
지갑을 호텔에 두고 왔어요. jigabeul hotere dugo wassoyo.	**I left my purse/wallet in the hotel.**
공항까지 가는 택시 좀 불러주시겠어요? gonghangkkaji ganeun taekssi jom bulrojusigessoyo?	**Could you call me a taxi to the airport?**
정말 감사합니다! 너무 즐겁게 보냈어요. jongmal gamsahamnida! nomu jeulgopkke bonaessoyo.	**Thank you very much! We had a very pleasant stay.**

Chapter 12. ASKING FOR DIRECTION (길 물어보기)

Listen to Track 66 (*Note: The chapter title pronunciation is included in this audio track.*)

저기요! jeogiyo!	**Excuse me!**
미안합니다. mianhamnida.	**I am sorry.**
길을 잃어버렸어요. gireul iroboryossoyo.	**I'm lost.**
길을 잃어버렸습니다. gireul iroboryotsseumnida.	**We're lost.**
어디로 가세요? odiro gaseyo?	**Where would you like to go?**
제가 지금 어디에 있는지 알려주실 수 있어요? jega jigeum odie inneunji alryojusil ssu issoyo?	**Can you tell me where am I now?**

친구들을 잃어버렸어요.
chingudeureul iroboryossoyo.

I have lost my friends.

호텔 주소를 못 찾겠어요.
hotel jusoreul mot chatkkessoyo.

I cannot find my hotel address.

놀이공원 가는 길 좀 알려주실 수 있나요?
norigongwon ganeun gil jom alryojusil ssu innayo?

Can you tell me the way to the amusement park?

성당에 가려면 어떻게 가야 돼요?
songdange garyomyon ottoke gaya dwaeyo?

How do I get to the cathedral?

식당/버스정류장/화장실 어디에 있어요?
sikttang/pposseujongnyujang/ hwajangsil odie issoyo?

Where can I find a restaurant/ bus stop/restroom?

이 지역 잘 아세요?
i jiyok jal aseyo?

Do you know this area well?

Listen to Track 67

이 길이 (location) 가는 길 맞나요?
i giri (location) ganeun gil mannayo?

Is this the right way to (location)?

이 거리를 찾고 있어요.
i gorireul chatkko issoyo.

I'm looking for this street.

이 길로 가세요.
i gilro gaseyo.

Go this way.

바로 저기예요.
baro jogieyo.

It's over there.

직진하세요.
jikjjinhaseyo.

Go straight.

횡단보도를 건너세요.
hwengdanbodoreul gonnoseyo.

Cross the crosswalk.

길 끝에서요.
gil kkeutesoyo.

At the end of the road.

모퉁이에 있어요.
motungie issoyo.

It's on the corner.

여기에서 두 블록이에요.
yogieso du beulrogieyo.

It's two blocks from here.

앞으로 곧장 가시면 돼요.
apeuro gotjjang gasimyon dwaeyo.

It's straight ahead.

다음 거리에서 좌회전하세요.
daeum gorieso jwahwejonhaseyo.

Turn left at the next street.

신호등에서 우회전하세요.
sinhodeungeso uhwejonhaseyo.

Turn right at the traffic lights.

교차로까지 계속 직진하세요.
gyocharokkaji gyesok jikjjinhaseyo.

Keep going straight until the intersection.

Listen to Track 68

지도에서 위치 좀 알려 주실 수 있어요?
jidoeso wichi jom alryo jusil ssu issoyo?

Can you show me on the map?

얼마나 멀어요?
olmana moroyo?

How far is it?

여기에서 멀어요?
yogieso moroyo?

Is it far from here?

아주 가까워요.
aju gakkawoyo.

It's very close.

거기까지 걸어갈 수 있나요?
gogikkaji gorogal ssu innayo?

Can we walk there?

걸어가기에는 너무 멀어요.
gorogagieneun nomu moroyo.

It's too far to walk.

걸어서 몇 킬로예요?
goroso myot kilroeyo?

How many kilometers is the walk?

지름길이 있나요?
jireumkkiri innayo?

Is there a shortcut?

네, 있어요.
ne, issoyo.

Yes, there is.

지름길은 없어요.
jireumkkireun opssoyo.

There is no shortcut.

도와주셔서 감사합니다.
dowajusyoso gamsahamnida.

Thank you for your help.

별말씀을요.
byolmalsseumeulryo.

You are welcome.

Chapter 13. HOSPITAL/PHARMACY (병원/약국)

Listen to Track 69 (*Note: The chapter title pronunciation is included in this audio track.*)

AT THE HOSPITAL / 병원에서

가장 가까운 병원이 어디예요? gajang gakkaun byongwoni odieyo?	**Where is the nearest hospital / doctor's office?**
병원에 데려다 주세요. byongwone deryoda juseyo.	**Please bring me to the hospital/ clinic.**
구급차 좀 불러주세요. gugeupcha jom bulrojuseyo.	**Please call an ambulance.**
의사 좀 불러주세요. uisa jom bulrojuseyo.	**Please call a doctor.**
진찰을 받고 싶어요. jinchareul batkko sipoyo.	**I'd like to see a doctor.**
영어 하는 의사가 필요해요. yongo haneun uisaga piryohaeyo.	**I need a doctor who speaks English.**

여자 의사한테 진찰받을 수 있나요? yoja uisahante jinchal badeul ssu innayo?	**Could I see a female doctor?**
예약 하셨나요? yeyak hasyonnayo?	**Do you have an appointment?**
예약하고 싶어요. yeyakago sipoyo.	**I'd like to make an appointment.**
응급상황입니다. eunggeupssanghwangimnida.	**It's an emergency.**
무엇을 도와드릴까요? muoseul dowadeurilkkayo?	**How can I help you?**

Listen to Track 70

어디가 안 좋으세요? odiga an joeuseyo?	**What's the problem?**
몸이 어때요? momi ottaeyo?	**How are you feeling?**
아파요. / 몸이 안 좋아요. apayo. / momi an joayo.	**I'm sick. / I'm not feeling well.**
두통이 있어요. dutongi issoyo.	**I have a headache.**
저는 임산부예요. joneun imsanbueyo.	**I'm pregnant.**
부상당했어요. busangdanghaessoyo.	**I have an injury.**
너무 아파요. nomu apayo.	**I'm in a lot of pain.**
다리에 통증이 있어요. darie tongjjeungi issoyo.	**I've got a pain in my legs.**
숨쉬기가 힘들어요. sumswigiga himdeuroyo.	**I'm having difficulty breathing.**
저는 …이/가 있어요. joneun …i/ga issoyo.	**I have (a/an) …**

천식 cheonsig	**asthma**

Listen to Track 71

기관지염 gigwanjiyeom	**bronchitis**
변비 byeonbi	**constipation**
기침 gichim	**cough**
설사 seolsa	**diarrhea**
심장 질환 simjang jilhwan	**heart condition**
메스꺼움 meseukkeoum	**nausea**
인후통 inhutong	**sore throat**
치통 chitong	**toothache**
그러신지 얼마나 되셨어요? geurosinji olmana dwesyossoyo?	**How long have you been feeling like this?**
혹시 알레르기 있으세요? hokssi alrereugi isseuseyo?	**Do you have any allergies?**

Listen to Track 72

저는 ⋯ 알레르기가 있어요. joneun ... alrereugiga issoyo.	**I am allergic ...**
항생제에⋯ hangsaengjee...	**... to antibiotics**
소염제에⋯ soyomjee...	**... to anti-inflammatories**

아스피린에⋯ aseupirine...	... to aspirin
벌침에⋯ bolchime...	... to bee stings
진통제에⋯ jintongjee...	... to codeine
페니실린에⋯ penisilrine...	... to penicillin
약은 먹고 있어요? yageun mokkko issoyo?	Are you taking any medicine?
(name of medicine) 을/를 먹고 있어요. (name of medicine) eul/reul mokkko issoyo.	I'm taking (name of medicine).
체온 잴게요. cheon jaelkkeyo.	Let me take your body temperature.
혈압 잴게요. hyorap jaelkkeyo.	Let me take your blood pressure.
혈액 검사 받아야 돼요. hyoraek gomsa badaya dwaeyo.	You need to have a blood test.
엑스레이 찍어야 돼요. eksseurei jjigoya dwaeyo.	You need to have an x-ray.

Listen to Track 73

수술해야 돼요. susul haeya dwaeyo.	We need to do a surgery.
주사 놓 게요. jusa noeulkkeyo.	I'm going to give you an injection.
휴식이 필요해요. hyusigi piryohaeyo.	You need rest.
처방전 드릴게요. chobangjon deurilkkeyo.	I will give you a prescription.

하루에 몇 번 먹어야 하나요? harue myot bon mogoya hanayo?	**How many times a day do I take it?**
하루에 한 번/두 번/세 번 식후에 드세요. harue han bon/du bon/se bon sikue deuseyo.	**Please take it once/twice/three times a day after a meal.**
증상이 지속되면 다시 오세요. jeungsangi jisokttwemyon dasi oseyo.	**Come back again if symptoms persist.**
얼마예요? olmaeyo?	**How much will it be?**
의료보험 있어요? uiryobohom issoyo?	**Do you have medical insurance?**
보험 때문에 영수증이 필요해요. bohom ttaemune yongsujeungi piryohaeyo.	**I need a receipt for the insurance.**

Listen to Track 74

AT THE PHARMACY / 약국에서

해열제 좀 주세요. haeyoljje jom juseyo.	**I'd like some paracetamol.**
…약 좀 주시겠어요? ...yak jom jusigessoyo?	**Can you give me something for...?**
두통… dutong...	**... a headache?**
멀미… molmi...	**... car sickness?**
독감… dokkkam...	**... flu?**
설사… solssa...	**... diarrhea?**
화상… hwasang...	**... sunburn?**

Listen to Track 75

이 약 있어요? i yak issoyo?	**Do you have this medicine?**
처방전 있으세요? chobangjon isseuseyo?	**Do you have a prescription?**
의사한테 처방전 받았어요. uisahante chobangjon badassoyo.	**I've got a prescription here from the doctor.**
처방전 없이 살 수 있나요? chobangjon opssi sal ssu innayo?	**Can I buy this without a prescription?**
처방전이 있어야만 살 수 있어요. chobangjoni issoyaman sal ssu issoyo.	**It's only available by prescription.**
부작용이 있나요? bujagyongi innayo?	**Does it have any side-effects?**
구급상자를 사고 싶어요. gugeupssangjareul sago sipoyo.	**I would like to buy a first-aid kit.**
선크림 있어요? sonkeurim issoyo?	**Do you sell sunblock?**
소독용 알코올 있어요? sodogyong alkool issoyo?	**Do you sell rubbing alcohol?**
모기약 있어요? mogiyak issoyo?	**Do you have anything for mosquito bites?**
어린이한테 안전한가요? orinihante anjonhangayo?	**Is it safe for kids?**

Chapter 14. TOURIST ATTRACTION (관광지)

Listen to Track 76 (*Note: The chapter title pronunciation is included in this audio track.*)

관광 안내소가 어디예요? gwangwang annaesoga odieyo?	**Where is the tourist office?**
저희는 (location)에 가고 싶어요. johineun (location)e gago sipoyo.	**We'd like to go to (location).**
여기서 유명한 관광지는 어디예요?? yogiso yumyonghan gwangwangjineun odieyo?	**What are the famous tourist spots here?**
이 지역에서 방문할 만한 곳이 어디예요? i jiyogeso bangmunhal manhan gosi odieyo?	**What is there to visit in the area?**
이 근처에 해변이 있나요? i geunchoe haebyoni innayo?	**Are there any beaches near here?**
낚시할 수 있는 곳이 어디예요? nakssihal ssu inneun gosi odieyo?	**Where can I go fishing?**
아이들이 할만한 게 있나요? aideuri halmanhan ge innayo?	**Is there anything for children to do?**

한국 지도를 사고 싶어요.
hanguk jidoreul sago sipoyo.

I would like to buy a map of Korea.

안내 책자 있어요?
annae chaekjja issoyo?

Do you have any brochures?

시티 투어 있나요?
ssiti tuo innayo?

Is there a city tour?

단체 여행 코스가 있나요?
danche yohaeng kosseuga innayo?

Are there any group tours?

Listen to Track 77

시간 당 가격이 얼마예요?
sigan dang gagyogi olmaeyo?

What is the charge per hour?

입장료가 얼마예요?
ipjjangnyoga olmaeyo?

How much does it cost to get in?

입장료가 포함되어 있나요?
ipjjangnyoga pohamdweo innayo?

Is the admission fee included?

음식/교통/숙박이 포함되어 있나요?
eumsik/gyotong/sukppagi
pohamdweo innayo?

Is food/transportation/ accommodation included?

어린이 할인 있어요?
orini harin issoyo?

Is there a discount for children?

경로 할인 있어요?
gyongno harin issoyo?

Is there a discount for senior citizens?

이 여행은 얼마나 걸려요?
i yohaengeun olmana golryoyo?

How long is the tour?

가이드가 포함되어 있나요?
gaideuga pohamdweo innayo?

Does it include a tour guide?

영어 가이드를 원해요.
yongo gaideureul wonhaeyo.

I want a tourist guide who speaks English.

박물관 보러 가고 싶어요.
bangmulgwan boro gago sipoyo.

I'd like to see the museum.

박물관 안내 책자 있어요?
bangmulgwan annae chaekjja issoyo?

Do you have brochures with information about the museum?

저는 조각에 관심이 있어요.
joneun jogage gwansimi issoyo.

I am interested in sculpture.

저는 그림에 관심이 있어요.
joneun geurime gwansimi issoyo.

I am interested in painting.

Listen to Track 78

몇 시에 열어요?
myot sie yoroyo?

What time do you open?

입구가 어디예요?
ipkkuga odieyo?

Where is the entrance?

입장료가 얼마예요?
ipjjangnyoga olmaeyo?

How much is admission?

음식이나 음료를 가지고 들어갈 수
있나요?
eumsigina eumnyoreul gajigo deurogal
ssu innayo?

Can I bring in food or drinks?

사진/동영상 촬영이 가능한가요?
sajin/dongyongsang chwaryongi
ganeunghangayo?

**Am I allowed to take photos/
videos?**

사진 좀 찍어 주시겠어요?
sajin jom jjigo jusigessoyo?

**Can you please take a picture of
me?**

만져 봐도 돼요?
manjo bwado dwaeyo?

Can I touch it?

만지면 안 돼요.
manjimyon an dwaeyo.

You can't touch it.

저건 뭐예요?
jogon mwoeyo?

What is that?

기념품을 사고 싶어요.
ginyompumeul sago sipoyo.

I'd like to buy some souvenirs.

몇 시에 닫아요?
myot sie dadayo?

What time do you close?

출구가 어디예요?
chulguga odieyo?

Where is the exit?

Listen to Track 79

다음 투어는 언제예요? daeum tuoneun onjeeyo?	**When's the next tour?**
가장 가까운 해변이 어디예요? gajang gakkaun haebyoni odieyo?	**Where is the nearest beach?**
여기에서 수영해도 안전해요? yogieso suyonghaedo anjonhaeyo?	**Is it safe to swim here?**
안전하지 않아요. 저는 추천 안 해요. anjonhaji anayo. joneun chuchon an haeyo.	**It's not safe. I don't recommend it.**
여기 물은 깨끗한가요? yogi mureun kkaekkeutangayo?	**Is the water clean here?**
이 해변에 안전 요원 있나요? i haebyone anjon yowon innayo?	**Is there a lifeguard on this beach?**
음악회에 가고 싶어요. eumakwee gago sipoyo.	**I would like to go to a concert.**
저는 음악 듣기를 아주 좋아해요. joneun eumak deutkkireul aju joahaeyo.	**I love listening to music.**
지금 갈 수 있는 좋은 콘서트 있어요? jigeum gal ssu inneun joeun konssoteu issoyo?	**Are there any good concerts on?**
클래식 음악은/재즈는 어디에서 들을 수 있어요? keulraesik eumageunjjaejeuneun odieso deureul ssu issoyo?	**Where can we hear some classical music / jazz?**
춤 추려면 어디로 가야 돼요? chum churyomyon odiro gaya dwaeyo?	**Where can we go to dance?**
콘서트 표는 어디에서 사요? konssoteu pyoneun odieso sayo?	**Where can I buy tickets for the concert?**
오늘 밤 표로 두 장 부탁드려요. oneul bam pyoro du jang butaktteuryoyo.	**I'd like two tickets for tonight.**

Chapter 15. WEATHER AND SEASON (날씨와 계절)

Listen to Track 80 (*Note: The chapter title pronunciation is included in this audio track.*)

날씨 어때요? nalssi ottaeyo?	**What's the weather like?**
오늘 날씨 어때요? oneul nalssi ottaeyo?	**How's the weather today?**
날씨 좋아요. nalssi ottaeyo.	**The weather is nice.**
하늘이 맑아요. haneuri malgayo.	**The sky is clear.**
화창해요. hwachanghaeyo.	**It's sunny.**
따뜻해요. ttatteutaeyo.	**It's warm.**
더워요. dowoyo.	**It's hot.**

흐려요.
heuryoyo.

It's cloudy.

추워요.
chuwoyo.

It's cold.

바람 불어요.
baram buroyo.

It's windy.

비 와요.
bi wayo.

It's raining.

눈 와요.
nun wayo.

It's snowing.

안에 있읍시다.
ane isseupssida.

Let's stay inside.

Listen to Track 81

몇 도예요?
myot doeyo?

What's the temperature?

30도 정도예요.
samsiptto jongdoeyo.

It's around 30 degrees. (celsius)

영하예요.
yonghaeyo.

It's below freezing.

오늘 일기예보 어때요?
oneul ilgiyebo ottaeyo?

How's the forecast today?

하루 종일 맑을 거예요.
haru jongil malgeul kkoeyo.

It will be sunny the whole day.

비 올 거예요.
bi ol kkoeyo.

It's going to rain.

천둥번개 칠 거예요.
chondungbongae chil kkoeyo.

There will be a thunderstorm.

한국의 계절은 어때요?
hanguge gyejoreun ottaeyo?

What are the seasons in Korea?

한국은 지금 무슨 계절이에요?
hangugeun jigeum museun gyejorieyo?

What season is it now in Korea?

봄 bom	spring
여름 yoreum	summer
가을 gaeul	autumn
겨울 gyoul	winter

한국에서 날씨가 가장 좋은 달은 몇 월이에요?
hangugeso nalssiga gajang joeun dareun myot worieyo?

What months have the best weather in Korea?

Chapter 16. EMOTIONS (감정들)

Listen to Track 82 (*Note: The chapter title pronunciation is included in this audio track.*)

오늘 기분이 어때요? oneul gibuni ottaeyo?	**How are you feeling today?**
좋으면 좋겠어요. joeumyon jokessoyo.	**I hope you are fine.**
저 오늘 기분 좋아요. jo oneul gibun joayo.	**I am feeling good today.**
지금 너무 행복해요. jigeum nomu haengbokaeyo.	**I'm very happy right now.**
더 이상 행복할 수 없을 것 같아요. do isang haengbokal ssu opsseul kkot gatayo.	**I don't think I can be any happier right now.**
신나요. sinnayo.	**I feel excited.**
좋네요. jonneyo.	**That's good.**

기분이 왜 그렇게 좋아요?
gibuni wae geuroke joayo?

Why are you so happy?

무슨 좋은 일 있어요?
museun joeun il issoyo?

Did something good happen?

(name)씨는요?
(name)ssineunnyo?

How about you, (name)?

괜찮아요?
gwaenchanayo?

Are you okay?

조금 슬퍼요.
jogeum seulpoyo.

I feel a little sad.

걱정돼요.
gokjjongdwaeyo.

I'm worried.

너무 슬퍼하지 마요.
nomu seulpohaji mayo

Don't be so sad.

Listen to Track 83

힘든 하루였어요.
himdeun haruyossoyo.

It's been a difficult day.

저 지금 기분 안 좋아요.
jo jigeum gibun an joayo.

I'm in a bad mood.

오늘 엄청 우울해요.
oneul omchong uulhaeyo.

I feel very depressed today.

무슨 일이에요?
museun irieyo?

What's going on?

뭐가 잘못됐어요?
mwoga jalmotttwaessoyo?

What's wrong?

뭐가 문제예요?
mwoga munjeeyo?

What's the matter?

저한테 얘기해 보세요.
johante yaegihae boseyo.

Please tell me about it.

뭐 때문에 화났어요?
mwo ttaemune hwanassoyo?

What are you angry about?

왜 그렇게 생각하세요?
wae geuroke saenggakaseyo?

Why do you think so?

남편이 저를 너무 화나게 했어요.
nampyoni joreul nomu hwanage haessoyo.

My husband made me very angry.

저는 그 사람 태도에 화가 나요.
joneun geu saram taedoe hwaga nayo.

I'm mad at his behavior.

마음이 안 좋네요.
maeumi an jonneyo.

Sorry to hear that.

걱정하지 마세요, 다 잘 될 거예요.
gokjjonghaji maseyo. da jal dwel kkoeyo.

Don't worry, everything will be fine.

저도 그러길 바라요.
jodo geurogil barayo.

I hope so.

곧 알게 될 거예요.
got alge dwel kkoeyo.

We'll see.

Chapter 17. AT WORK (직장에서)

Listen to Track 84 (*Note: The chapter title pronunciation is included in this audio track.*)

저는 이 자리에 관심이 있어요. joneun i jarie gwansimi issoyo.	**I'm interested in this position.**
저는 이 일에 지원하고 싶어요. joneun i ire jiwonhago sipoyo.	**I'd like to apply for this job.**
임시직이에요, 아니면 정규직이에요? imsijigieyo, animyon jonggyujigieyo?	**Is this a temporary or permanent position?**
근무 시간이 어떻게 돼요? geunmu sigani ottoke dwaeyo?	**What are the working hours?**
급여가 어떻게 돼요? geubyoga ottoke dwaeyo?	**What's the salary for the job?**
어느 분께 보고해야 돼요? oneu bunkke bogohaeya dwaeyo?	**Who would I report to?**
제가 그 일 하고 싶어요. jega geu il hago sipoyo.	**I'd like to take the job.**

언제 시작할까요? onje sijakalkkayo?	**When do you want me to start?**
여기서 일한 지 얼마나 됐어요? yogiso ilhan ji olmana dwaessoyo?	**How long have you worked here?**
저는 신입 사원입니다. joneun sinip sawonimnida.	**I'm a new employee.**

Listen to Track 85

매니저님 어디에 계세요? maenijonim odie gyeseyo?	**Where is the manager?**
회의 중이십니다. hwei jungisimnida.	**He's in a meeting.**
회의 몇 시에 시작해요? hwei myot sie sijakaeyo?	**What time does the meeting start?**
회의 몇 시에 끝나요? hwei myot sie kkeunnayo?	**What time does the meeting finish?**
보고서를 볼 수 있을까요? bogosoreul bol ssu isseulkkayo?	**Can I see the report?**
판매 보고서 여기 있습니다. panmae bogoso yogi itsseumnida.	**Here's the sales report.**
실행 계획을 승인해 주세요. silhaeng gyehwegeul seunginhae juseyo.	**Please approve the action plan.**
제 컴퓨터에 문제가 있어요. je kompyutoe munjega issoyo.	**There's a problem with my computer.**
인터넷 연결이 끊어졌어요. intonet yongyori kkeunojossoyo.	**The internet is disconnected.**
제 이메일을 사용할 수 없어요. je imeireul sayonghal ssu opssoyo.	**I can't use my email.**

Listen to Track 86

프린터가 작동하지 않아요. peurintoga jakttonghaji anayo.	**The printer isn't working.**
잠깐 쉽시다. jamkkan swipssida.	**Let's take a quick break.**
한 시간 뒤에 다시 시작합시다. han sigan dwie dasi sijakapssida.	**Let's start again in an hour.**
저 점심시간에 외출할 거예요. jo jomsimsigane wechulhal kkoeyo.	**I'm going out for lunch break.**
한 시간 후에 돌아올게요. han sigan hue doraolkkeyo.	**I'll be back after an hour.**
오늘 하루 어땠어요? oneul haru ottaessoyo?	**How's today been for you?**
주말에계획 있어요? jumare gyehwek issoyo?	**Do you have any plans for the weekend?**
함께 일하게 돼서 기뻐요. hamkke ilhage dwaeso gippoyo.	**I'm happy to work with you.**
저 퇴근해요. jo twegeunhaeyo.	**I'm off work.**
내일 봐요. naeil bwayo.	**See you tomorrow.**

Chapter 18. POLICE STATION (경찰서)

Listen to Track 87 (*Note: The chapter title pronunciation is included in this audio track.*)

경찰서가 어디에 있어요? gyongchalssoga odie issoyo?	**Where is the police station?**
경찰에 전화할 거예요. gyongchare jonhwahal kkoeyo.	**I will call the police.**
경찰하고 이야기하고 싶어요. gyongchalhago iyagihago sipoyo.	**I want to speak to a policewoman.**
실례합니다. 도움이 필요해요. silryehamnida. doumi piryohaeyo.	**Excuse me, sir. I need help.**
긴급상황이에요. gingeupssanghwangieyo.	**It's an emergency.**
무엇을 도와드릴까요? muoseul dowadeurilkkayo?	**What can I do for you?**
도난 신고를 하고 싶어요. donan singoreul hago sipoyo.	**I want to report a theft.**

강도를 당했어요. gangdoreul danghaessoyo.	**I've been robbed.**
카메라를 도난당했어요. kamerareul donandanghaessoyo.	**My camera was stolen.**
배낭을 도둑맞았어요. baenangeul dodungmajassoyo.	**My backpack was stolen.**

Listen to Track 88

제 차를 도난당했어요. je chareul donandanghaessoyo.	**My car has been broken into.**
제 아이가 실종됐어요. je aiga siljjongdwaessoyo.	**My child is missing.**
어떻게 해야 돼요? ottoke haeya dwaeyo?	**What should I do?**
길을 잃었어요. 제 호텔 찾는 것 좀 도와주실 수 있나요? gireul irossoyo je hotel channeun got jom dowajusil ssu innayo?	**I'm lost. Can you help me find my hotel?**
어느 호텔에서 묵고 있어요? oneu hotereso mukkko issoyo?	**Which hotel are you staying at?**
어쩌다 이렇게 됐어요? ojjoda iroke dwaessoyo?	**Where did it happen?**
제 아파트에서 일어난 일이에요. je apateueso ironan irieyo.	**It happened in my apartment.**
언제 일어난 일이에요? onje ironan irieyo?	**When did it happen?**
오늘 아침에 일어났어요. oneul achime ironassoyo.	**It happened this morning.**
그 사람의 얼굴을 봤나요? geu sarame olgureul bwannayo?	**Did you get a good look at the person?**
아니요, 못 봤어요. aniyo, mot bwassoyo.	**No, I did not see.**

네, 봤어요.
ne, bwassoyo.

Yes, I saw him.

Listen to Track 89

그 사람의 모습을 설명할 수 있어요?
geu sarame moseubeul solmyonghal
ssu issoyo?

Can you describe the person's appearance?

할 수 있어요.
hal ssu issoyo.

I can do that.

이 양식을 작성해 주세요.
i yangsigeul jakssonghae juseyo.

Please fill out this form.

진정하세요.
jinjeonghaseyo.

Be calm. / Calm down. / Take it easy.

저희가 할 수 있는 모든 것들을
하겠습니다.
johiga hal ssu inneun modeun
gottteureul hagetsseumnida.

We will do everything we can.

휴대폰 번호가 어떻게 되세요?
hyudaepon beonhoga ottoke dweseyo?

What's your mobile number?

전화 좀 하고 싶어요.
jonhwa jom hago sipoyo.

I'd like to make a phone call.

핸드폰 있어요?
haendeupon issoyo?

Do you have a mobile phone?

핸드폰 좀 사용할 수 있을까요?
haendeupon jom sayonghal ssu
isseulkkayo?

Can I use your mobile?

곧 연락드리겠습니다.
got yolraktteurigetsseumnida.

We will contact you soon.

걱정하지 마세요, 다 잘될 거예요.
gokjjonghaji maseyo. da jal dwel
kkoeyo.

Don't worry, everything is going to be okay.

Chapter 19. FRIENDS (친구들)

* Note : Depending on your relationship with your friend, you can use formal speech or casual speech. In this chapter, we will look at the phrases in casual speech used by close friends.

Listen to Track 90 (*Note: The chapter title pronunciation is included in this audio track.*)

안녕! 반가워. annyong! bangawo.	**Hey! Good to see you.**
나도. nado.	**You too.**
우리 오랫동안 못 봤다. uri oraetttongan mot bwattta.	**We haven't seen each other for a long time.**
오랜만이야. oraenmaniya.	**Long time no see.**
너무 보고 싶었어. nomu bogo siposso.	**I missed you so much.**
다시 만나서 기뻐. dasi mannaso gippo.	**I'm glad to see you again.**

요즘 어때?
yojeum ottae?

How are things?

잘 지내?
jal jinae?

How are you?

어떻게 지냈어?
ottoke jinaesso?

How've you been?

잘 지내고 있어.
jal jinaego isso.

I'm doing well.

Listen to Track 91

너는 어때?
noneun ottae?

What about you?

나는 좋아.
naneun joa.

I'm great.

무슨 새로운 소식 있어?
museun saeroun sosik isso?

What's new with you?

요즘 뭐 해?
yojeum mwo hae?

What are you doing these days?

나는 얼마 전에 취업했어.
naneun olma jone chwiopaesso.

I just got a job.

좋다. 잘 됐다.
jota. jal dwaettta.

That's nice. Good for you.

나는 일이 바빠. 너는?
naneun iri bappa. noneun?

I'm busy at work. You?

나도 그래. 새 직장은 어때?
nado geurae. sae jikjjangeun ottae?

Same here. How's your new job?

괜찮아. 배울 게 많아.
gwaenchana. baeul kke mana.

It's okay. There's a lot to learn.

Listen to Track 92

나는 지금 마케팅 회사에서 일하고 있어. naneun jigeum maketing hwesaeso ilhago isso.	I'm now working in a marketing company.
점심 먹자. jeomsim meogja.	Let's have lunch.
오늘 밤에 술 마시러 가자. oneul bame sul masiro gaja.	Let's go grab a drink tonight.
오늘 재밌었어. 고마워. oneul jaemissotkko gomawosso.	Thanks for today. I had fun.
또 만나자. tto mannaja.	Let's meet up again.
당연하지, 전화해. dangyonhaji, jonhwahae.	Sure, give me a call.
안녕, 곧 보자. annyeong, got boja.	Bye, see you soon.
다음에 볼 때까지 잘 지내. daeume bol ttaekkaji jal jinae.	Take care until we meet next time.

Chapter 20. DATING AND ROMANCE (데이트와 로맨스)

Listen to Track 93 (*Note: The chapter title pronunciation is included in this audio track.*)

데이트할래요? deiteuhalraeyo?	**Do you want to go on a date?**
저랑 사귈래요? jorang sagwilraeyo?	**Will you go out with me?**
좋아요! joayo!	**I'd love to!**
내일 저녁에 만나요. naeil jonyoge mannayo.	**Let's meet tomorrow evening.**
제가 데리러 갈게요. jega deriro galkkeyo.	**I will pick you up.**
오늘 멋있어요. oneul mosidoyo.	**You look great today.**
오늘 너무 예뻐요. oneul nomu yeppoyo.	**You look very pretty today.**

칭찬 고마워요!
chingchan gomawoyo!

Thanks for the compliment!

저녁 어디에서 먹고 싶어요?
jonyok odieso mokkko sipoyo?

Where do you want to have dinner?

저 괜찮은 식당 알아요.
jo gwaenchaneun sikttang arayo.

I know a great restaurant.

Listen to Track 94

저 사랑에 빠지고 있어요.
jo sarange ppajigo issoyo.

I'm falling in love with you.

좋아해요.
joahaeyo.

I like you.

사랑해요.
saranghaeyo.

I love you.

저도 사랑해요.
jodo saranghaeyo.

I love you too.

첫눈에 반했어요.
chonnune banhaessoyo.

It was love at first sight.

제 여자친구/남자친구가 되고 싶어요?
je yojachingunamjachinguga dwego sipoyo?

Do you want to be my girlfriend/ boyfriend?

우리 잘 어울려요.
uli jal oulryoyo.

We look good together.

손 잡아도 돼요?
son jabado dwaeyo?

May I hold your hand?

제 인생에 와줘서 고마워요.
je insaenge wajwoso gomawoyo.

Thank you for coming into my life.

같이 좋은 시간 보낼 수 있어서 너무 좋아요.
gachi joeun sigan bonael ssu issoso nomu joayo.

I love to have a good time together with you.

Listen to Track 95

집까지 데려다 줄게요. jipkkaji deryoda julkkeyo.	**Let me take you home.**
집까지 태워다 줄게요. jipkkaji taewoda julkkeyo.	**I'll give you a ride home.**
언제 또 만날 수 있어요? onje tto mannal ssu issoyo?	**When can I see you again?**
문자해줄래요? munjjahaejulraeyo?	**Can you text me?**
연락할게요. yolrakalkkeyo.	**I will call you.**
전화할게요. jonhwahalkkeyo.	**I will give you a call.**
고마워요, 즐거운 시간이었어요. gomawoyo, jeulgoun siganiossoyo.	**Thanks, I had a great time.**
즐거웠어요. jeulgowossoyo.	**I had a good time.**

Chapter 21. FAMILY AND RELATIVES (가족 및 친척)

Listen to Track 96 (*Note: The chapter title pronunciation is included in this audio track.*)

제 가족이에요. je gajogieyo.	**This is my family.**
이 분은 제... / 이 분들은 제... 이에요/예요. i buneun je... / i bundeureun je... ieyo/ yeyo.	**This is my... / These are my...**
남편 nampyeon	**husband**
부인/아내 buin/anae	**wife**
엄마 omma	**mom**
아빠 appa	**dad**

어머니 omoni	mother
아버지 aboji	father
부모님 bumonim	parents
언니 onni	older sister
오빠 oppa	older brother
여동생 yodongsaeng	younger sister
남동생 namdongsaeng	younger brother
자매 jamae	sister
형제 hyongje	brother
남매 nammae	siblings

Listen to Track 97

딸 ttal	daughter
아들 adeul	son
아이들/자녀 aideul/janyo	children
이모, 고모 imo(mom side), gomo(dad side)	aunt
삼촌 samchon	uncle

조카 joka	**niece, nephew**
사촌 sachon	**cousin**
할머니, 외할머니 halmoni (dad side), wehalmoni (mom side)	**grandmother**
할아버지, 외할아버지 haraboji (dad side), weharaboji (mom side)	**grandfather**
새엄마 saeomma	**stepmom**
새아빠 saeappa	**stepdad**

Listen to Track 98

이복자매 ibokjjamae	**stepsister**
이복형제 ibokyongje	**stepbrother**
시댁, 처가 sidaek (husband's family), choga (wife's family)	**family-in-law**
시어머니, 장모님 siomoni (a husband's mother), jangmonim (a wife's mother)	**mother-in-law**
시아버지, 장인어른 siaboji (a husband's father), janginoreun (a wife's father)	**father-in-law**
사위 sawi	**son-in-law**
며느리 myoneuri	**daughter-in-law**

가족이 몇 명이에요?
gajogi myot myongieyo?

How many are you in the family?

대가족이에요?
daegajogieyo?

Do you have a big family?

저희는 대가족이에요.
johineun daegajogieyo.

We have a big family.

저희 가족은 작아요.
johi gajogeun jagayo.

My family is small.

저, 엄마, 아빠만 있어요.
jo, omma, appaman issoyo.

It's just me, my mom, and my dad.

자녀 있으세요?
janyo isseuseyo?

Do you have kids?

3살짜리 딸 하나 있어요.
sesaljjari ttal hana issoyo.

I have a 3-year-old daughter.

Listen to Track 99

형제가 몇 명이에요?
hyongjega myot myongieyo?

How many brothers and sisters do you have?

오빠 한 명하고 여동생 두 명 있어요.
oppa han myonghago yodongsaeng du myong issoyo.

I've got one older brother and two younger sisters.

막내/맏이예요?
mangnae/majieyo?

Are you the youngest/eldest?

저는 막내/맏이예요.
joneun mangnae/majieyo.

I am the youngest/eldest.

큰누나는 18살이에요.
keunnunaneun yolryodolssarieyo.

My big sister is 18 years old.

제 남동생은 6살 돼요.
je namdongsaengeun yosotssal dwaeyo.

My little brother is turning 6.

저희 부모님은 60세가 넘으셨어요.
johi bumonnimeun yukssipssega
nomeusyossoyo.

My parents are over 60 years old.

저희 아빠는 갈색 눈이에요.
johi appaneun galssaek nunieyo.

My dad has brown eyes.

저랑 아버지는 많이 닮았어요.
jorang abojineun mani dalmassoyo.

Like father, like son.

가족이 어때요?
gajogi ottaeyo?

What's your family like?

저희 가족은 아주 친해요.
johi gajogeun aju chinhaeyo.

My family is very close.

저희는 정말 다 잘 지내요.
johineun jongmal da jal jinaeyo.

We all get along really well.

Chapter 22. MONEY AND BANKING (돈과 은행)

Listen to Track 100 (*Note: The chapter title pronunciation is included in this audio track.*)

저 현금이 없어요. jo hyongeumi opssoyo.	**I don't have any cash.**
저 돈을 좀 인출해야 돼요. jo doneul jom inchulhaeya dwaeyo.	**I need to withdraw some money.**
제일 가까운 ATM은 어디 있어요? jeil gakkaun anmeueun odi issoyo?	**Where is the nearest ATM?**
쇼핑 센터에 있어요 ssyoping ssentoe issoyo.	**There is one in the shopping center.**
이 ATM 어떻게 사용하는지 모르겠어요. i ATM ottoke sayonghaneunji moreugessoyo.	**I don't understand how to use this ATM.**
어떻게 해야 돼요? ottoke haeya dwaeyo?	**What do I have to do?**

여기에 카드를 넣어야 돼요. yogie kadeureul nooya dwaeyo.	You need to insert your card in here.
핀 번호를 입력해야 돼요. pin bonhoreul imnyokaeya dwaeyo.	You need to enter your PIN number.
다음에 뭐 해야 돼요? daeume mwo haeya dwaeyo?	What do I have to do next?
원하는 옵션을 클릭하면 완료돼요. wonhaneun opssyoneul keulrikamyon walryodwaeyo.	Click on whichever option you want, and you're done.
성공했어요. 고맙습니다. songgonghaessoyo. gomapsseumnida.	I succeeded. Thank you.
한국 원화가 없어요. hanguk wonhwaga opssoyo.	I don't have Korean won.
달러/유로밖에 없어요. ttalro/yurobakke opssoyo.	I only have dollars/euros.

Listen to Track 101

돈 어디에서 바꿀 수 있어요? don odieso bakkul ssu issoyo?	Where can I change some money?
가장 가까운 환전소는 어디예요? gajang gakkaun hwanjonsoneun odieyo?	Where is the nearest foreign exchange office?
잔돈으로 바꿔 줄 수 있으세요? jandoneuro bakkwo jul ssu isseuseyo?	Can you change this for me?
환율이 어떻게 돼요? hwanyuri ottoke dwaeyo?	What is the exchange rate?
1달러에 1,300원이에요. ilttalroe chonsambaegwonieyo.	One dollar is 1,300 won.
500달러 환전하고 싶어요. obaekttalro hwanjonhago sipoyo.	I´d like to exchange 500 US dollars, please.
제일 가까운 은행이 어디예요? jeil gakkaun eunhaengi odieyo?	Where is the nearest bank?

은행 몇 시에 열어요?
eunhaeng myot sie yoroyo?

When does the bank open?

은행 몇 시에 닫아요?
eunhaeng myot sie dadayo?

When does the bank close?

국민은행에 오신 것을 환영합니다.
gungmineunhaenge osin goseul
hwanyonghamnida.

Welcome to Kookmin Bank.

무엇을 도와 드릴까요?
muoseul dowa deurilkkayo?

What can I do for you?

돈을 좀 인출해야 돼요.
doneul jom inchulhaeya dwaeyo.

I need to withdraw some money.

Listen to Track 102

계좌 정보 알려주시겠어요?
gyejwa jongbo alryojusigessoyo?

Can I please have your account details?

네, 여기 제 통장이고 계좌번호
안에 있어요.
ne yogi je tongjangigo gyejwabonho
ane issoyo.

Yes, here is my passbook and it has the account number inside.

얼마나 꺼내시겠어요?
olmana kkonaesigessoyo?

How much would you like to take out?

500달러 인출할 거예요.
obaekttalro inchulhal kkoeyo.

I need to withdraw $500.

어느 계좌에서 인출하시겠어요?
oneu gyejwaeso inchulhasigessoyo?

Which account would you like to take it from?

제 예금 계좌에서요.
je yegeum gyejwaesoyo.

From my savings account.

큰돈 말고 작은 돈으로 주세요.
keundon malgo jageun doneuro juseyo.

Small bills, please.

잔돈으로 주시겠어요?
jandoneuro jusigessoyo?

May I have some change?

수수료는 얼마예요?
susuryoneun olmaeyo?

What's the charge for that?

5,000원입니다. ochonwonimnida.	**It's 5,000 won.**
무료입니다. muryoimnida.	**It's free of charge.**
더 필요한 건 없으세요? do piryohan gon opsseuseyo?	**Do you need anything else?**
아니요, 없어요. 이 안녕히 계세요. aniyo, opssoyo. annyonghi gyeseyo.	**No, I don't. Goodbye.**

Chapter 23: Miscellaneous (기타 다양한 표현)

Listen to Track 103 (*Note: The chapter title pronunciation is included in this audio track.*)

Chapter 23.1: Quantity (양)

⋯ 500밀리리터 ... obaek milririto	**500 milliliters of ...**
⋯ 1리터 ... il rito	**a liter of ...**
⋯ 반 병 ... ban byong	**half bottle of ...**
⋯ 한 병 ... han byeong	**a bottle of ...**
⋯ 한 컵 ... han keob	**a glass of ...**
... 한 잔 ... han jan	**a cup/mug/shot of...**
... 100그램 ... baek guraem	**100 grams of ...**

··· 500그램 ... obaek geuraem	**500 grams of ...**
... 1킬로 ... il killo	**a kilo of ...**
... 한 조각 ... han jogag	**a slice of ...**
... 일부 ... ilbu	**a portion of ...**

Listen to Track 104

수십 ··· susib ...	**a dozen ...**
... 한 상자... han sangja	**a box of ...**
··· 한 봉지 ... han bongji	**a bag of ...**
··· 한 병 ... han byong	**a jar of ....**
... 4분의 1 ... sabune il	**a quarter of ...**
10 퍼센트 (10%) sip posenteu (10%)	**ten percent**
더 deo	**more**
덜 deol	**less**
충분한 chungbunhan	**enough**
두 배 du bae	**double**
두 번 du beon	**twice**

한 번
han beon

once

Listen to Track 105

Chapter 23.2-1: Sino-Korean Numbers (숫자)

영/공 yong/gong	0
일 il	1
이 i	2
삼 sam	3
사 sa	4
오 o	5
육 yug	6
칠 chil	7
팔 pal	8
구 gu	9
십 sib	10
십일 sibil	11
십이 sibi	12

십삼
sipssam

13

Listen to Track 106

십사 sipssa	**14**
십오 sibo	**15**
십육 simnyuk	**16**
십칠 sipchil	**17**
십팔 sippal	**18**
십구 sipkku	**19**
이십 isib	**20**
이십일 isibil	**21**
이십이 isibi	**22**
이십삼 isipssam	**23**
삼십 samsib	**30**
삼십일 samsibil	**31**
삼십이 samsibi	**32**
사십 sasib	**40**

사십일 sasibil	**41**
사십이 sasibi	**42**
오십 osib	**50**
육십 yugsib	**60**
칠십 chilsib	**70**
칠십일 chilsibil	**71**
칠십이 chilsibi	**72**
팔십 palsib	**80**
팔십일 palsibil	**81**
팔십이 palsibi	**82**
구십 gusib	**90**
구십일 gusibil	**91**
백 baeg	**100**
백십 baegsib	**110**
이백 ibaeg	**200**
이백오십 ibaegosib	**250**

천 cheon	**1,000**
백만 baegman	**one million**

Listen to Track 107

Chapter 23.2-2: Native Korean Numbers (숫자)

하나 hana	**1**
둘 dul	**2**
셋 set	**3**
넷 net	**4**
다섯 dasot	**5**
여섯 yosot	**6**
일곱 ilgop	**7**
여덟 yodol	**8**
아홉 ahop	**9**
열 yol	**10**
열하나 yolhana	**11**
열둘 yoldul	**12**

마흔둘 maheundul	**42**
쉰 swin	**50**
예순 yesun	**60**
일흔 ilheun	**70**
일흔하나 ilheunhana	**71**
일흔둘 ilheundul	**72**
여든 yodeun	**80**
여든하나 yodeunhana	**81**
여든둘 yodeundul	**82**
아흔 aheun	**90**
아흔하나 aheunhana	**91**
아흔아홉 aheunahop	**99**

Listen to Track 108

Chapter 23.3: Asking and Telling Time and Frequency (시간과 빈도 묻고 말하기)

몇 시예요? myot sieyo?	**What time is it?**
지금... jigeum...	**Now it's...**

두 시예요 du sieyo	**two o'clock**
세 시예요 se sieyo	**three o'clock**
여섯 시예요 yosot sieyo	**six o'clock**
밤 12시예요. / 자정이에요. bam yolttusieyo. / jajongieyo.	**It's midnight.**
9시 10분이에요. ahopssi sipppunieyo.	**It is ten past nine.**
9시 15분이에요. ahopssi sibobunieyo.	**It is a quarter past nine.**
10시 25분 전이에요. / 9시 35 분이에요. yolssi isibobun jonieyo.. / ahopssi samsibobunieyo.	**It is 25 to ten. / It is 9:35.**
9시 45분이에요. ahopssi sasibobunieyo.	**It is a quarter to 10.**
10시 10분 전이에요. yolssi sipppun jonieyo.	**It is 10 to 10.**
언제 열어요/닫아요/시작해요/ 끝나요? onje yoroyo/dadayo/sijakaeyo/ kkeunnayo?	**When does it open/close/begin/ finish?**
3시에요. sesieyo.	**At three o'clock.**
3시 전에요. sesi joneyo.	**Before three o'clock.**
3시 후에요. sesi hueyo.	**After three o'clock.**

Listen to Track 109

Chapter 23.4: Days of the Week (한 주의 날)

월요일 woryoil	**Monday**
화요일 hwayoil	**Tuesday**
수요일 suyoil	**Wednesday**
목요일 mogyoil	**Thursday**
금요일 geumyoil	**Friday**
토요일 toyoil	**Saturday**
일요일 ilyoil	**Sunday**
오늘 oneul	today
내일 naeil	**tomorrow**
어제 eoje	yesterday
그제 / 그저께 geuje / geujokke	**the day before yesterday**
모레 molae	**the day after tomorrow**
오늘 밤 oneulppam	**tonight**
어젯밤 ojetppam	**last night**
이번 주 ibon ju	**this week**

다음 주 daeum ju	**next week**
지난 주 jinan ju	**last week**
오전 ojon	**the morning, a.m**
오후 ohu	**the afternoon, p.m**
아침 achim	**the morning, breakfast**
점심 jomsim	**midday, lunch**
저녁 jonyok	**the evening, dinner**
밤 bam	**the night**
새벽 saebyok	**the dawn**

Listen to Track 110

Chapter 23.5: Months of the Year (한 해의 달)

1월 ilwol	**January**
2월 iwol	**February**
3월 samwol	**March**
4월 sawol	**April**
5월 owol	**May**

6월 yuwol	**June**
7월 chirwol	**July**
8월 parwol	**August**
9월 guwol	**September**
10월 siwol	**October**
11월 sibirwol	**November**
12월 sibiwol	**December**

Listen to Track 111

Chapter 23.6: Colors and Shapes (색깔과 모양)

빨간색 ppalgansaeg	**red**
주황색 juhwangsaeg	**orange**
노란색 nolansaeg	**yellow**
초록색 chorokssaek	**green**
파란색 paransaek	**blue**
남색 namsaek	**indigo**
보라색 borasaek	**purple**

하늘색 haneulssaek	sky blue
분홍색 bunhongsaek	pink
흰색 hinsaek	white
회색 hwesaek	grey
갈색 galssaek	brown
검은색 gomeunsaek	black
무지개색 mujigaesaek	rainbow color
동그라미/원형 donggeurami/wonhyong	circle
타원형 tawonhyong	oval
세모/삼각형 semo/samgakyong	triangle
네모/사각형 nemo/sagakyong	tetragon
정사각형 jongsagakyong	square
직사각형 jikssagakyong	rectangle
오각형 ogakyong	pentagon
육각형 yukkkakyong	hexagon
팔각형 palgakyong	octagon

정육면체 jongyungmyonche	**cube**
하트 모양 hateu moyang	**heart shape**
별 모양 byol moyang	**star shape**
달 모양 dal moyang	**moon shape**

Conclusion

Korean is an incredibly beautiful language to learn. Whether you're learning these phrases as a way to boost your Korean language studies or to help you enjoy your Korean holiday, we hope this book was able to help you achieve your goals.

If you wish to further your studies in Korean language, we have other books available at FluentinKorean.com and on Amazon. Please feel free to browse the different titles. The books, such as Korean Grammar for Beginners and Korean Short Stories, will help improve your reading and listening skills.

Thank you for sticking with us all the way to the end! We hope you got a lot out of this book! We'd love to hear what you think. If you have comments, questions, or suggestions about this book, please let us know by sending us an email at support@ fluentinkorean.com. This will help us to enhance our books and provide you with better learning resources.

For more insights about the Korean language and culture, do visit our website at FluentinKorean.com. We are always working towards providing useful content for you.

And so with that, we say our goodbyes.

Thank you,

Fluent in Korean Team

The audio files need to be accessed online. No worries though—it's easy!

On your computer, smartphone, iPhone/iPad, or tablet, simply go to this link:

https://fluentinkorean.com/phrasebook-audio/

Be careful! If you are going to type the URL on your browser, please make sure to enter it completely and exactly. Otherwise, it will lead you to an incorrect web page.

You should be directed to a web page where you can see the cover of your book.

Below the cover, you will find two "Click here to download the audio" buttons in blue and orange color.

Option 1 (via Google Drive): The blue one will take you to a Google Drive folder. It will allow you to listen to the audio files online or download them from there. Just "Right click" on the track and click "Download." You can also download all the tracks in one click—just look for the "Download all" option.

Option 2 (direct download): The orange button/backup link will allow you to directly download all the files (in .zip format) to your computer.

Note: This is a large file. Do not open it until your browser tells you that it has completed the download successfully (usually a few minutes on a broadband connection, but if your connection is slow it could take longer).

The .zip file will be found in your "Downloads" folder unless you have changed your settings. Extract the .zip file and you will now see all the audio tracks. Save them to your preferred folder or copy them to your other devices. Please play the audio files using a music/Mp3 application.

Did you have any problems downloading the audio? If you did, feel free to send an email to support@fluentinkorean.com. We'll do our best to assist you, but we would greatly appreciate it if you could thoroughly review the instructions first.

Thank you,

Fluent in Korean Team

About Fluent in Korean

FluentinKorean.com believes that Korean can be learned almost painlessly with the help of a learning habit. Through its website and the books and audiobooks that it offers, Korean language learners are treated to high-quality materials that are designed to keep them motivated until they reach their language learning goals. Keep learning Korean and enjoy the learning process with books and audio from Fluent in Korean.

FluentinKorean.com is a website created to help busy learners learn Korean. It is designed to provide a fun and fresh take on learning Korean through:

- Helping you create a daily learning habit that you will stick to until you reach fluency, and
- Making learning Korean as enjoyable as possible for people of all ages.

With the help of awesome content and tried-and-tested language learning methods, Fluent in Korean aims to be the best place on the web to learn Korean.

The website is continuously updated with free resources and useful materials to help you learn Korean. This includes grammar and vocabulary lessons plus culture topics to help you thrive in a Korean-speaking location—perfect not only for those who wish to learn Korean but also for travelers planning to visit Korean-speaking destinations.

For any questions, please email support@fluentinkorean.com.

Your opinion counts!

If you enjoyed this book, please consider leaving a review on Amazon and help other language learners discover it.

Scan the QR code below:

Visit the link below:

https://geni.us/seEH

Made in the USA
Las Vegas, NV
30 September 2024